未命名｜艺术 ·1

主编：孙长江

Waking & Making

河南大学出版社
HENAN UNIVERSITY PRESS
·郑州·

图书在版编目（CIP）数据

未命名艺术. 1 ： 汉文、英文 / 孙长江主编.
郑州 ： 河南大学出版社, 2025. 4. -- ISBN 978-7-5649-6282-1

Ⅰ. K825.7

中国国家版本馆 CIP 数据核字第 2025A621G3 号

未命名艺术 . 1

WEI MING MING YISHU. 1

主　　编　孙长江
责任编辑　时　海
责任校对　李　云
装帧设计　王利锋

出　　版　河南大学出版社
　　　　　地址：郑州市郑东新区商务外环中华大厦 2401 号　邮编：450046
　　　　　电话：0371-86059701（营销部）
网　　址　hupress.henu.edu.cn
制　　作　太原市一方设计有限公司
印　　刷　深圳市新联美术印刷有限公司
版　　次　2025 年 4 月第 1 版
印　　次　2025 年 4 月第 1 次印刷
开　　本　1/16
印　　张　12.25
字　　数　300 千字
定　　价　198.00 元

序言

过去的时代，艺术家将灵光乍现记录在画布和纸张上，千头万绪到最后总会编织成一个主题。于是灵感化为具象的“作品”。也有艺术家选择独坐书斋，不想在世人面前抛头露面。他们主动隐去自己的姓名，好奇之人想要挖掘创作趣事，却在“佚名”和“无题”前止步。

数字时代，艺术家习惯在电脑上敲下文字，制作图像，生成影像……灵感以比特的形式永远储存了下来。计算机上新建的文档，系统会自动生成“未命名”。当偶然和例外被提纯为某种艺术观念，“未命名”就会被“命名”取代。

“未命名”意味着一种艺术创作的时态，它既可以记录稍纵即逝的即兴创作，也可以留存苦思冥想后难以被语言定义的灵韵。

在更广阔的艺术社会学立场上，初出茅庐的艺术家们在艺术市场上籍籍无名，也尚未被艺术评论家们提及，他们以一种“未命名”的身份和姿态，或肆意或真诚地释放着蓬勃的想象力。

混乱、青涩、真诚、质朴、偏激、反叛……这些词语无法涵盖作为某种艺术情境的“未命名”的所有可能性。时间之矢终会让“未命名”变成过去时，尚待命名的创作者也总是被时代指认。我们能做的，就是在艺术进入更复杂的经纬之前，保留这份珍贵的创造和勇气。这就是《未命名》艺术书系创立的初衷。

《未命名》艺术书系的第一辑邀请了九位青年创作者，他们各有专长，分享了油画、版画、雕塑、装置、公共艺术等领域的真诚创作。这些采访文字经过了主编的编辑加工，删去了访谈中没有必要的社交辞令。

将艺术家完整的创作观念和创作过程呈现在读者面前是一项艰巨的任务。即便如此，《未命名》编辑团队也努力以一种真实质朴的风格，最大程度地保留创作者想象力的火种。每一位读者的参与和关注，都有可能促成新的交流和对话，这也恰恰是艺术赖以生存的土壤。我们真挚地希望本书系能为记录中国艺术的创作尽一份绵薄之力，也期盼它能更多地激发起读者对艺术的热望。

主编：孙长江

Editor's Note

In times past, artists recorded their eureka moments on canvas and paper, and thousands of ideas were always woven into a single theme in the end. Inspiration was then transformed into figurative "works".

There are artists who prefer seclusion in their creations, hiding away from the public eye. They take the initiative to conceal their names, leaving curious minds that want to dig into the anecdotes to halt before the mysterious "Anonymous" and "Untitled".

In this digital era, artists find comfort in the rhythmic tapping of keys, crafting words, composing images, and giving birth to visuals on their electronic canvases... Thus, long live their inspiration, taking the form of bits.

Whenever a new document is created on a computer, the system automatically labels it as "Untitled". However, if serendipity and exception be narrated into any distinct artistic conception, the "Untitled" yields its reign to a carefully chosen name.

The word "untitled" implies a momentary phase in artistic creation. It can either symbolize a fleeting instancy of improvisation or the ineffable spirit from an artist's profound contemplation that can barely be defined by words.

From a broader perspective of art sociology, the emerging artists, who are unknown in the art market and have not yet been touched by any art critics, are letting their vibrant imagination run in an "Untitled" manner, regardless their recklessness or integrity.

Chaos, youthfulness, sincerity, simplicity, radicalism, rebellion... These vocabularies cannot encompass all the possibilities for any vibrant Waking&Making artistic contexts. The arrow of time will eventually turn the "Untitled" into a past tense, and the Waking&Making Artists yet to be named will always be identified by the passage of times. What we can do, before art enters a world of complex dimensions, is to preserve the lionhearted creativity and determination of these Waking&Making Artists. And this is the original intention behind the founding of the Waking&Making.

The inaugural issue of the Waking&Making features nine young creators, each with their own specialties, sharing sincere creations from the fields of oil painting, printmaking, sculpture, installation, public art, and more. The interview texts have been carefully edited by the editor-in-chief, and unnecessary social pleasantries have been deleted.

It is a difficult task to present the artists' complete creative concept and creation process to the readers. Even so, the editorial team of the Waking&Making endeavors to preserve the spark of imagination in the creators to the greatest possible extent with an authentic approach. The attention and concern of every reader have the potential to facilitate new exchanges and dialogues, which creates the very soil that art thrives on. We hope sincerely that Waking&Making will contribute in some small way to the documentation of artistic creation in China, and that it will inspire in readers a greater passion for art.

Editor-in-Chief
Sun Changjiang

35

https://s.mj.run/Qg5k0bIv8cQ An animal with a superfluous horn::8 growing from its back Renaissance copperplate engraving style::8, side view fiction alien scientific illustrations 32k uhd realistic detailing, lith printinganimal species tetrapods horns on a hill an ancient animal with horns large horns large mammoth enlivened grisaille antarctic theropod animal [illegible] Image #2

目录 CONTENTS

宁诗涵

NING SHIHAN

01

我在做了这么多关于"艺术介入社会"的驻地项目和公共艺术之后，发现艺术不会也不能直接对症下药，解决社会问题，但它可以发现隐藏在现实背后的社会议题或者矛盾……

After undertaking numerous residency projects and public art related to "art intervention in society", I've realized that art cannot and should not directly cure social problems. However, it can uncover social issues or contradictions hidden behind reality...

02

杨懿

YANG YI

之前听到一首歌，歌词里一个人跟一个机器人对话。那个人说，"我真的可以成为自己想成为的人吗？"机器人说，"当然可以，但是如果你这么想的话可能就不太行。"所以不要犹豫，直接去做就好。

I heard a song before with lyrics featuring a conversation between a person and a robot. The person asked, "Can I really become the person I want to be?" The robot said, "Of course, but if you think too much about it, it might not work." So, don't hesitate, just go and do it.

03

陈晓奎

CHEN XIAOKUI

没错，当你坚定下来要寻找某个东西，真的会不顾一切，我挺享受这其中的过程。人在全身心投入的时候会进入一种心流的状态，我感受到自己与整个世界连在一起……

Absolutely. When you're determined to find something, you'll go all out for it. I really enjoy the process. When you're fully immersed, you enter a state of flow, feeling connected to the entire world...

张浩迪

ZHANG HAODI

对我而言，
艺术就是恰好正在做喜欢的事情。
它对我的价值追求和思维方式是有影响的，
塑造了我现在的生活状态。

For me,
art is precisely doing something I love.
It influences my values and way of thinking,
shaping my state of life.

04

05

贾童童

JIA TONGTONG

我感觉艺术创作是循序渐进的，也许一开始就有了某种感觉，但是没有办法把它变成现实，用合适的媒介材料把它表现出来。它开始于一次精神上的挣扎，自相矛盾的情感……

I feel that artistic creation is gradual. Perhaps there's an initial sensation, but it's challenging to materialize it, to express it through the right medium and materials. It starts with a mental struggle, and contradictory emotions...

06

←徐艺翔 XU YIXIANG

当创作者都去思考什么是元宇宙，时间和精力自然偏向于概念，作品本身的接受度自然就大打折扣，这也是某种困境吧……

When creators are all thinking about what the metaverse is, their time and energy naturally lean towards concepts, so then the acceptance of the work itself would be undermined...

→王亚楠 WANG YANAN

……在碎片化时间中去做创作。我不会觉得这是一个难题，其实是必须要去经历的事情……

...doing creative work in fragmented time. I don't see it as a problem; it's something that must be experienced...

07

鲍文馨

BAO WENXIN

每一件艺术作品都是创作者对某种情感的表达，观众用自己的感官去接受这些信息，幸运的话，二者之间还会有强烈的感情共鸣……

Every piece of artwork is an expression of the creator's emotions. Audiences can engage with this information through their senses, and if fortunate, a strong emotional resonance could happen between the two...

08

张少语

ZHANG SHAOYU

表面上看，技术的确解放了人的双手，但艺术表达的难度却没有因此减少。马塞尔 · 杜尚、约瑟夫 · 博伊斯都是制作现成品艺术的大师，但在他们之后，“人人都是艺术家”的时代似乎并没有到来……

At first glance, technology has indeed freed human hands, but the difficulty of expressing artistically has not diminished as a result. Masters like Marcel Duchamp and Joseph Beuys were experts in creating ready-made art. However, after them, the era of "everyone is an artist" seems not to have arrived...

艺术不是良方，是药引

ART IS NOT A CURE, BUT A PRESCRIPTION

HUABAO

宁诗涵：我所学的专业是公共艺术，因为疫情的原因，一直受限在固定的地点，无法去体验新的空间。2023 年初，我的导师带我在上海驻地半年，参加“上海城市空间艺术季”。那段时间我每天与上海的居民以及很多艺术家打交道，这次经历对我产生了很大影响，让我对人与人、人与社会的关系，有了更深入的理解。

Ning Shihan: My academic focus is on public art. Due to pandemic restrictions, I had been confined to fixed locations, and was unable to explore new spaces. In early 2023, my mentor took me to Shanghai for a six-month residency, participating in the *Shanghai Urban Space Art Season* exhibition. During that time, daily interactions with Shanghai residents and numerous artists profoundly influenced my perspective. This experience deepened my understanding of interpersonal and societal relationships.

倪家桥社区居民白大爷
Mr. Bai, a resident of Nijiaqiao Community

未命名　艺术与公共生活真正发生交互的部分在哪儿?

宁　我的毕业作品以“艺术介入”的方式呈现，其实也跟上海的“城市空间艺术季”有关。当时我认识了策展人张晋，他也来自成都。他告诉我成都市玉林南路有一个社区更新项目，政府想与艺术家合作，做一些有公共价值的探索。

倪家桥社区始建于上世纪八十年代，之前名为“青春岛社区”。建筑的风貌已经非常老旧了，随着新一轮城市化的建设，这样的社区空间逐渐破败，宜居性也大大降低。我的童年也在类似的小区中度过，这个项目唤醒了我的记忆，所以我决定留下来，为它做点什么。

W&M　Where do you think the interaction between art and public life truly occurs?

Ning　My graduation project, presented through “art intervention”, is closely tied to the *Shanghai Urban Space Art Season* exhibition. I connected with curator of the exhibition, Zhang Jin, who is also from Chengdu. He informed me about a community renewal project on Yulin South Road in Chengdu, where the government sought collaboration with artists for explorations with public value.

The Nijiaqiao Community, originally named the “Qingchun Island Community”, was established in the 1980s. The aging appearance of the buildings and the impact of new urbanization led to the gradual deterioration of the community’s livability. Having spent my childhood in a similar community, this project stirred my memories, prompting me to stay and contribute.

未命名　驻地的这段时间，你都做了哪些准备工作?

宁　在完成《第六频道》之前，我花了 3 个月左右的时间，每天与居民相处，近距离观察和体验他们的生活，留下了大量的记录影像和田野调查的文字。由于展览的空间有限，最后呈现在作品当中的内容是精简过的。不过我更在意的是“艺术介入”的过程，而不是最终的结果。

政府计划把倪家桥社区居民区的两侧改造成一个文化步行街，新增一些咖啡厅和美术馆。策展团队根据社区自身的历史，以及城市发展的需要，计划增设一个社区美术馆。也许，《第六频道》的归宿就是回到这个美术馆。

W&M　During your residency, what preparations did you undertake?

Ning　Before completing *The Sixth Channel*, I spent about three months daily interacting with other residents, closely observing and experiencing their lives. This period left me with extensive visual records and notes from field investigations. Due to limited exhibition space, the content presented in the artwork was streamlined. However, my primary focus lies on the process of “art intervention” rather than the final result.

The government plans to transform both sides of the Nijiaqiao Community’s residential area into a cultural pedestrian street, incorporating cafés and art galleries. The curatorial team plans to establish a community art museum based on the community’s history and the city’s developmental needs. Perhaps, *The Sixth Channel* will eventually find its home in this museum.

未命名 **某种意义上，《第六频道》变成了倪家桥社区历史记忆的一部分。**

宁 对，这个艺术项目是一个三到五年的长期驻地项目，所以有机会的话，我也希望未来在这个社区里做更多的创作，延续《第六频道》的创作和我的观察。

W&M In a sense, *The Sixth Channel* has become part of the Nijiaqiao Community's historical memory, right?

Ning Yes, this art project is a three to five-year long-term residency endeavor. If given the opportunity, I hope to continue creating more within this community, extending the creation of *The Sixth Channel* and my observations.

拆除中的倪家桥社区
The Nijiaqiao Community under demolition

未命名 **不管是驻地创作，还是与美术馆合作，你的经验似乎证明，你对当下的展览市场有自己成熟的判断，与策展人的沟通也更为顺畅。**

宁 这是我的兴趣使然吧！读了硕士之后，我的创作视野不再局限于探索物质媒介的可能，我感兴趣的是媒介背后的真实生活。

《第六频道》这件作品其实在学院的标准里，并没有得到老师的完全认可。他们可能更喜欢物质化、视觉观赏性高的作品。

毕业展览结束后，我参加了由社交媒体“小红书”举办的“青年发光艺术展”。在展览上，《三联生活周刊》对我进行了采访。学院外的艺术生态对年轻艺术家的接受度和包容度超出了我的想象。收到这些积极的反馈，的确让我很惊喜。

如果《第六频道》只放在美术馆或者画廊展出，接收到的评价可能仅仅来自于艺术界。对于艺术世界的体系，我也不是很明白，现在的我，也只能在边缘观望。

而在社交媒体上，对艺术品的评价就完全多元化了。也许这些评价有好有坏，但是对我而言，艺术家受到关注，真的是一个很期冀的事情。通过艺术家，大家就可以去关注装置艺术背后的社区，以及它所承载的历史记忆。

W&M Whether in residency creation or collaborating with museums, your experience seems to prove your mature judgment of the current exhibition market, and your communication with curators seems quite smooth.

Ning I'm driven by my interests! After completing my master's degree, my creative vision expanded beyond exploring the possibilities of material mediums. I became interested in the real-life stories behind the mediums.

Actually, *The Sixth Channel* didn't receive full recognition from my teachers based on the academy's standards. They might have preferred works that were more materialized and visually appealing.

After the graduation exhibition, I participated in the *Youth Shining Art Exhibition* hosted by the social media platform Rednote. During the exhibition, *Sanlian Lifeweek* interviewed me. The acceptance and inclusiveness of the art environment outside the academy exceeded my expectations. Receiving such positive feedback genuinely surprised me.

If *The Sixth Channel* were only exhibited in a museum or gallery, the feedback might have come only from the art world. I don't fully understand how the art world works, and currently, I can only observe from the sidelines.

On social media, evaluations of artworks are diverse. Perhaps these evaluations can be both positive and negative, but for me, people paying attention to an artist like me is something to look forward to. Through one artist, people can pay attention to the community behind installation art and the historical memories it carries.

未命名 **学院的评价与大众的反馈之间形成了一种反差，你怎么看待这种分歧？**

宁 对我的创作而言，大多数时间我都在跟人打交道，在体验和融入社区生活。正是有了这些经历，才有最后艺术化的呈现。“艺术介入”的前提是真实的生活，在这个语境里，艺术无法与生活相分离。我觉得大众认可我，也是基于这个原因吧。

W&M There seems to be a contrast between the academy's evaluation and the public's feedback on your work. How do you perceive this divergence?

Ning For my creations, most of the time, I engage with people, experiencing and immersing myself in community life. It's these experiences that lead to the final artistic presentation. The premise of "art intervention" is real life, and in this context, art cannot be separated from life. I think the public's recognition of me is based on this reason.

南门记忆地图（1956-70）
Nanmen Memory Map (1956-70)

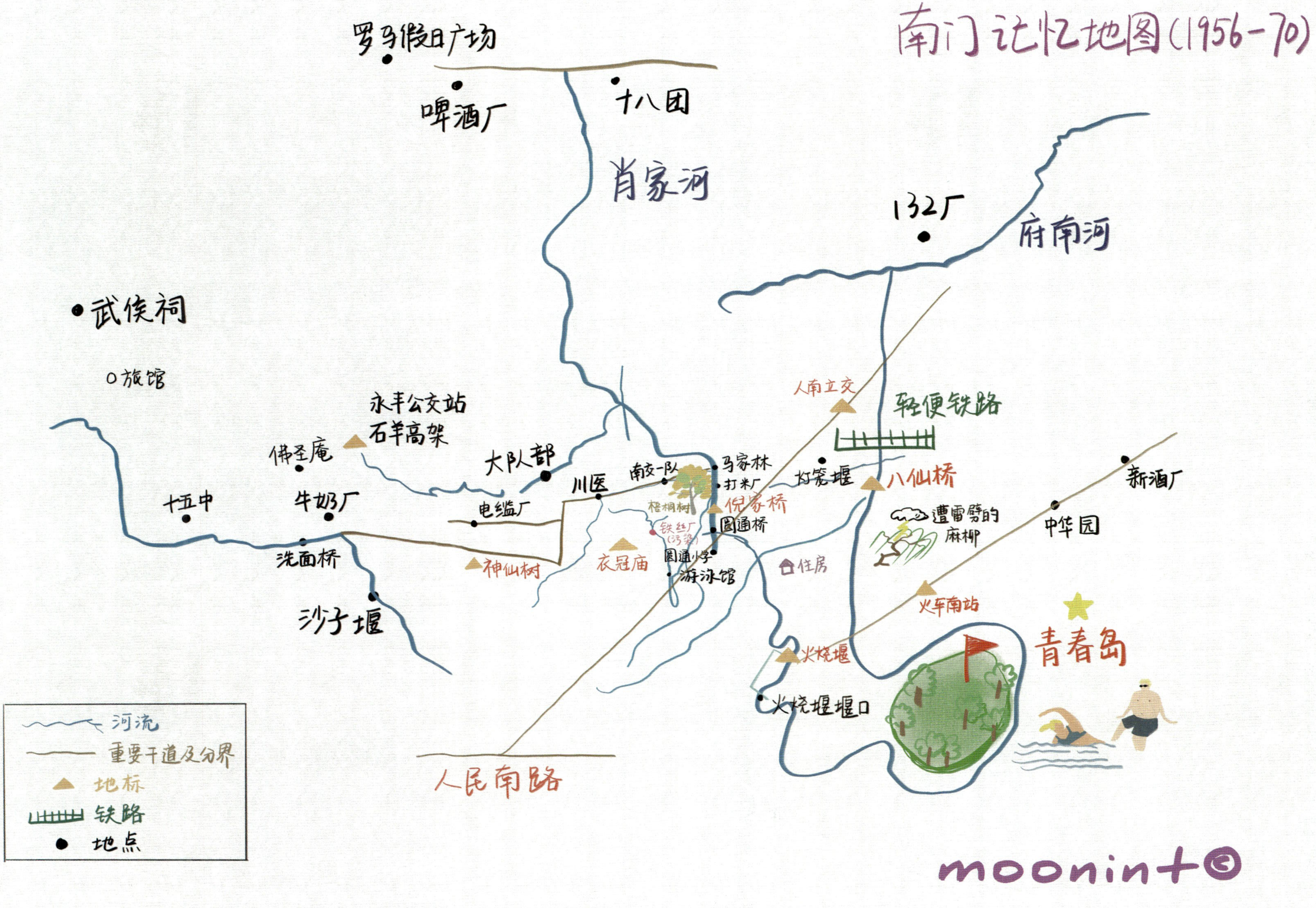

南门记忆地图(1956-70)
罗马假日广场
啤酒厂
十八团
肖家河
132厂
府南河
武侯祠
旅馆
永丰公交站
石羊高架
佛圣庵
大队部
十五中
牛奶厂
洗面桥
沙子堰
电缆厂
神仙树
川医
南交一队
梧桐树
铁丝厂(污染)
衣冠庙
马家林
打米厂
倪家桥
圆通桥
圆通小学
游泳馆
人南立交
轻便铁路
灯笼堰
八仙桥
遭雷劈的麻柳
住房
新酒厂
中华园
火车南站
火烧堰
火烧堰堰口
青春岛
人民南路
河流
重要干道及分界
地标
铁路
地点
moonint

未命名 **《第六频道》并不是在讲述你自己的个体经验，而是表达了更多的社会关注。**

宁 进入到真正的艺术创作，其实还是从自我出发的。不过，创作的过程肯定包含着对周遭世界的感受。社交网络中涌现出一些从来没有学过艺术的人，但是他们对艺术的感受力却超过了学艺术的人。

我在做了这么多关于“艺术介入社会”的驻地项目和公共艺术之后，发现艺术不会也不能直接对症下药，解决社会问题，但它可以发现隐藏在现实背后的社会议题或者矛盾，这是我做创作最希望看到的东西。

W&M So *The Sixth Channel* isn't just about your individual experience; it expresses broader social concerns.

Ning Entering into genuine artistic creation begins with the self. However, the process of creation inevitably includes perceptions of the surrounding world. Social media has brought forth individuals who, despite never having studied art, possess a sensitivity to art that surpasses that of some art students.

After undertaking numerous residency projects and public art related to “art intervention in society”, I've realized that art cannot and should not directly cure social problems. However, it can uncover social issues or contradictions hidden behind reality. This is what I most hope to see in my creative work.

《第六频道》
The Sixth Channel

未命名 **《第六频道》是一件非常复杂的作品，它有特别多的维度，脚手架、防尘网、电视机、藤椅、收音机，循环播放的影像和声音，以及用 ChatGPT 写的小说。这些部分是如何组织在一起的？**

宁 起初，很多人看我的作品是被人工智能的声音吸引过来的。我在田野调查的时候，也是被一种特殊的声音所吸引。

社区改造的时候会产生很多噪音，居民们就生活在这个嘈杂的环境中。我漫步在社区，我好多次听到收音机发射出的声音与施工噪音混杂在一起。后来就找到了收音机的主人白大爷，他年近 80 岁，是一个土生土长的老成都人。

他是在我一筹莫展的时候出现的，与老人的聊天，让我慢慢了解了倪家桥社区的历史，以及成都市区的规划，这些都是鲜活的记忆。根据老人的描述，我还做了社区的图绘，很遗憾这部分内容没有展出，它能帮助我们更好地了解社区的历史。

防尘网和脚手架，这些是我每天都能看到的东西，它们代表着对过去的改造。电视机里播放的影像，时间线是递进的，记录了我第一次到社区调研，直至最后一次离开社区的轨迹。在居民们的日常视角中，最开始的时候只有简简单单的脚手架。之后，绿色的防尘网覆盖了整个居民楼，过去的历史与现实的互动被绿网隔开了。

为什么要把它呈现为一个像九宫格一样的东西？我觉得这种矩阵的感觉跟收音机频道的排列不谋而合，很像居民每天的生活状态，有一种被笼罩起来的感觉，被监视的感觉。

脚手架前面的几把椅子，也源自于真实生活。居民们不管噪音有多大，尘土有多飞扬，他们总是提着椅子，在茶余饭后聚在一起。除了情境的还原，椅子在我的作品里，也是希望观众与作品之间有一种对话的关系。

W&M *The Sixth Channel* is a very complex piece with various types of things—scaffolding, dust nets, televisions, rattan chairs, radios, looping images and sounds, and a novel written using ChatGPT. How are these elements organized together?

Ning Initially, many people were drawn to my work by the voice of artificial intelligence. During my field investigations, I was also captivated by a particular sound.

During community renovations, a lot of noise was generated, and residents lived in this noisy environment. While strolling through the community, I often heard radio broadcasts blending with construction noise. Later, I found the owner of the radio, Mr. Bai, who is nearly 80 years old and a native Chengdu resident.

He appeared when I was feeling at a loss, and our conversations gradually allowed me to understand the history of the Nijiaqiao Community and the urban planning of Chengdu. According to Mr. Bai's descriptions, I even created a community map, unfortunately not exhibited, which could have helped us better understand the community's history.

Dust nets and scaffolding, which I saw every day in that community during renovations, represent transformations from the past. The images played on the television follow a progressive timeline, documenting my first research visit to the community through to the final departure. From the residents' daily perspective, initially, there were simple scaffolding structures. Later, green dust nets covered the entire residential building, separating the interaction between past history and reality.

Why present it in a grid format like a tic-tac-toe board? I feel this grid-like sensation aligns with the arrangement of radio channels, mirroring the residents' daily life—a sense of being enveloped and monitored.

The chairs in front of the scaffolding also originate from real life. Regardless of the noise or dust, residents always carried chairs and gathered to chat after meals. Beyond situational reconstruction, the chairs in my work aim to establish a dialogue between the audience and the artwork.

《第六频道》局部

Detail of *The Sixth Channel*

未命名　与观众对话的设计是从一开始就有的吗？

宁　这个安排是作品做到最后才有的。脚手架、防尘网和老电视的九宫格组合，创造出了一种秩序感，但是整个作品显得太“规矩”了，有点僵硬。加上藤椅之后，能破一下这个方正的“形”。整个作品就有了一种对话的情境。收音机里的“第六频道”，也是为白大爷专门增加的，他喜欢听戏。

W&M　Did you plan to interact with the audience from the very beginning?

Ning　This arrangement emerged toward the end of creating the artwork. The tic-tac-toe combination of scaffolding, dust nets, and an old television creates a sense of order, but the entire work seemed too “square” and somewhat rigid. With the addition of rattan chairs, it breaks the strict “form”. The entire artwork then takes on a conversational tone. The “Sixth Channel” on the radio was specifically added for Mr. Bai; he enjoys listening to local operas.

未命名　白大爷喜欢的是地方戏，按照老人的期待，“第六频道”播放的应该是地方戏，但是你却用了 AI 大模型生产出来的小说。这种小说的形式是未来主义的，而你的整个作品其实都在讲过去的事情。

宁　很多人都会有这样的疑问，人工智能的声音出现在世纪末的建筑和人文环境里，有一种巨大的割裂感。我其实尝试过使用四川茶馆里的话本，但是加进去有一种不和谐的感觉。后来使用人工智能生成的小说，其实来源于我当时的一个观察。

社区改造项目开始的时候，还入驻了一批纪录片导演，他们每天都在认真地记录着社区里发生的一切。充满未来感的无人机，每天都在破旧的小区上空盘旋，其实是很矛盾和割裂的。

W&M　Mr. Bai enjoys local operas, and according to his expectations, “The Sixth Channel” should play local operas. However, you created a novel generated by a large AI model for it to play. The form of the novel is futuristic, while your entire artwork actually discusses past events.

Ning　Many people indeed have this question—why the voice of artificial intelligence appears in the setting of architecture and humanities at the turn of the century, which creates such a profound sense of detachment. I actually tried using local scripts from Sichuan teahouses, but adding them felt discordant. Later, I used a novel generated by artificial intelligence and it was actually originated from my observations at that time.

At the beginning of the community renovation project, a group of documentary filmmakers settled in, diligently documenting everything happening in the community. The futuristic drones hovering over the dilapidated neighborhood every day created a contradictory and fragmented atmosphere.

未命名　**这是你擅长使用的一种艺术语言，要在一种秩序感里制造一些冲突和反叛。**

宁　这也跟我自己的感受力有关吧。成都是一个内陆城市，没有什么大江大河。在小说里，我把倪家桥社区设定为漂浮在海上的岛。现实世界中，这里是网红打卡地，聚集着很多文艺青年和诗人。所以小说的主人公登岛之后，就遇到了生活在那里的最后一位诗人。小说的内容本身是荒诞的，用人工智能的声音去朗诵这个文本，会增加它的荒诞意味。

W&M　This seems to be a kind of artistic language you excel in—creating conflict and rebellion within a sense of order.

Ning　It's also related to my own sensitivity. Chengdu is a landlocked city without major rivers. In the novel, I set the Nijiaqiao Community as an island floating on the sea. In reality, this place is a popular spot, attracting many artistic youth and poets. So, in the novel, after the protagonist arrives on the island, they encounter the last poet living there. The content of the novel itself is absurd, and using the voice of artificial intelligence to recite this text enhances its absurdity.

未命名　真实的社区与人工智能生成的小说之间存在着什么样的关联?

宁　在《第六频道》展出的时候，很多观众都不会仔细听小说的内容，但也有部分观众认为，小说才是这个作品的核心。这个反馈的确让我思考了很久。

白大爷跟我说，倪家桥社区以前叫青春岛社区，2013 年以后这个名字就停用了。2000 年之前，社区旁边有一条河，它有自己的生态系统，生活着一些独特的鱼类，比如青鳝。随着市政规划，这条河成为地下河，青鳝也不复存在了。

事情能够引起我们的想象，你说它真实存在吗，其实也无从考证，我只是从白大爷口中听闻了这些传说。

在生成这篇小说的时候，我给人工智能输入了很多限定条件。有一部分是白大爷有关青春岛的回忆，也有很多是人工智能的联想。当时修改了很多稿，最后的文本比我自己写的还要好。后来，我把这个小说拿给白大爷听，他问我这到底是不是青春岛，怎么有种似是非是的感觉。

W&M　What is the connection between the real community and the AI-generated novel?

Ning　During the exhibition of *The Sixth Channel*, many viewers didn't pay close attention to the content of the novel, but some thought that the novel was the core of the work. This feedback indeed made me reflect for a long time.

Mr. Bai told me that the Nijiaqiao Community used to be called Qingchun (Youth) Island Community, and this name was abandoned after 2013. Before 2000, there was a river next to the community with its own ecosystem, housing unique fish such as eels. Due to urban planning, this river became an underground waterway, and the eels disappeared.

These things can evoke our imagination, whether they truly existed is hard to verify. I only heard these stories from Mr. Bai.

When generating this novel, I inputted many constraints into the artificial intelligence. Some were Mr. Bai's memories of Qingchun Island, and many were the associations made by artificial intelligence. I made a lot of modifications at that time, and the final text was better than what I could have written myself. Later, I played this novel for Mr. Bai to listen to, and he asked me if this was really Qingchun Island, feeling a sense of ambiguity.

未命名　创作《第六频道》的时候，还遇到过什么困难吗?

宁　困难总是有的，但总体还算顺利。我之前在杭州读了七年的书，也在当地做了一些社区艺术项目的尝试，但是我觉得杭州的社区文化氛围不是很浓。每次我们去介入的时候，居民们会对我们有戒备。我觉得成都人的天性就很容易亲近，很好打交道。包括我在这个社区待了半年，去居民家吃饭也是很习以为常的一件事情，之前在杭州感觉就没有这么好的状态。当然也有可能是我们之前的方式有问题。

W&M　Were there any difficulties encountered during the creation of *The Sixth Channel*?

Ning　Difficulties are always present, but overall, the process went relatively smoothly. I had spent seven years studying in Hangzhou before and attempted some community art projects there, but I felt that Hangzhou's community cultural atmosphere wasn't very strong. Every time we tried to intervene with the community, the residents were cautious. I think people in Chengdu are naturally easygoing and easy to get along with. During my six months in this community, having meals at residents' homes was a common thing. I didn't feel this level of comfort in Hangzhou before. Of course, it could also be that our previous approach to intervention had some issues.

AUTO STOP

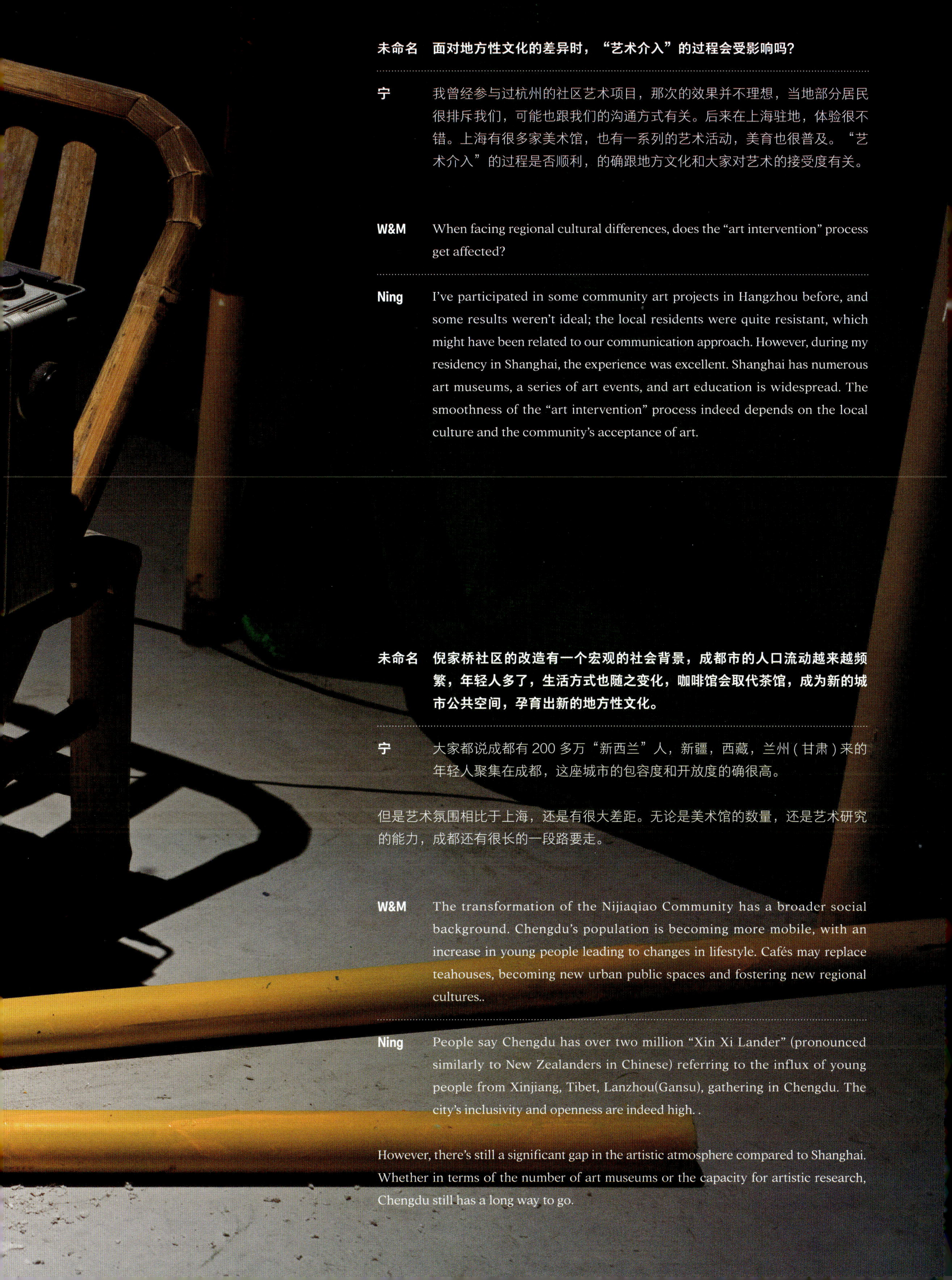

未命名　**面对地方性文化的差异时，“艺术介入”的过程会受影响吗？**

宁　我曾经参与过杭州的社区艺术项目，那次的效果并不理想，当地部分居民很排斥我们，可能也跟我们的沟通方式有关。后来在上海驻地，体验很不错。上海有很多家美术馆，也有一系列的艺术活动，美育也很普及。“艺术介入”的过程是否顺利，的确跟地方文化和大家对艺术的接受度有关。

W&M　When facing regional cultural differences, does the “art intervention” process get affected?

Ning　I’ve participated in some community art projects in Hangzhou before, and some results weren’t ideal; the local residents were quite resistant, which might have been related to our communication approach. However, during my residency in Shanghai, the experience was excellent. Shanghai has numerous art museums, a series of art events, and art education is widespread. The smoothness of the “art intervention” process indeed depends on the local culture and the community’s acceptance of art.

未命名　**倪家桥社区的改造有一个宏观的社会背景，成都市的人口流动越来越频繁，年轻人多了，生活方式也随之变化，咖啡馆会取代茶馆，成为新的城市公共空间，孕育出新的地方性文化。**

宁　大家都说成都有 200 多万“新西兰”人，新疆，西藏，兰州 (甘肃) 来的年轻人聚集在成都，这座城市的包容度和开放度的确很高。

但是艺术氛围相比于上海，还是有很大差距。无论是美术馆的数量，还是艺术研究的能力，成都还有很长的一段路要走。

W&M　The transformation of the Nijiaqiao Community has a broader social background. Chengdu’s population is becoming more mobile, with an increase in young people leading to changes in lifestyle. Cafés may replace teahouses, becoming new urban public spaces and fostering new regional cultures..

Ning　People say Chengdu has over two million “Xin Xi Lander” (pronounced similarly to New Zealanders in Chinese) referring to the influx of young people from Xinjiang, Tibet, Lanzhou(Gansu), gathering in Chengdu. The city’s inclusivity and openness are indeed high. .

However, there’s still a significant gap in the artistic atmosphere compared to Shanghai. Whether in terms of the number of art museums or the capacity for artistic research, Chengdu still has a long way to go.

未命名 **但是不是专业化的环境留给年轻艺术家的空间反倒不多？**

宁 我觉得不冲突。在成都做艺术，大家的第一印象是“野生”。成都有很多行为艺术家。我的朋友在春熙路，成都最繁华的步行街，做行为艺术，两个小时之后才有人干预。但是在上海或杭州，也许五分钟就会有人来打断你。成都已经有了艺术的土壤，但是缺乏一定的专业性，专业性可以让艺术走得更远一些。

W&M But is there much space left for young artists in an environment that is highly specialized?

Ning I don't think it's contradictory. Doing art in Chengdu, the first impression is "wild". Chengdu has many performance artists. My friend does performance art on Chunxi Road, the busiest pedestrian street in the city, and it takes two hours before anyone intervenes. But in Shanghai or Hangzhou, someone might interrupt you within five minutes. Chengdu already has the soil for art, but it lacks a certain level of professionalism. Professionalism can help art go much further.

未命名 **专业性总是与艺术理论和艺术史的教育挂钩。在你的创作过程中，其他艺术家的作品是否对你产生了影响？**

宁 对我的创作观念影响最大的人，其实是我的老师沈烈毅和石玩玩。他们让我知道，用艺术介入一个场域和社区的文化生态，最有说服力的往往是那些具体的个体和最接近微观层面的人和事物，而不是宏观展开的历史叙事。

W&M Professionalism is always linked to education in art theory and art history. In your creative process, have other artists' works influenced you?

Ning The people who have had the most significant impact on my creative concept are actually my teachers, Shen Lieyi and Shi Wanwan. They made me realize that the most convincing way to use art to intervene in the field and the cultural ecology of a community is often through specific individuals and things at the closest micro level, rather than grand historical narratives.

白大爷参观《第六频道》
Mr. Bai and *The Sixth Channel*

未命名　**白大爷的出现应该让你的创作观念得到了印证吧！**

宁　白大爷是一个很健谈的人，他是那一代老人的缩影，我从他身上知道了整个社区乃至成都的变迁史，说他是成都的活地图毫不为过。

W&M　I guess the appearance of Mr. Bai should have confirmed your creative concept!

Ning　Mr. Bai is a very talkative person; he is the epitome of that generation of elderly people. I learned about the entire history of the community and even the changes in Chengdu from him. Calling him a living map of Chengdu wouldn't be an exaggeration.

未命名　**你对《第六频道》最后呈现的效果满意吗？**

宁　我之前想做一个调频的收音机，频道内容都是可以让观众去调节和 DIY 的，让这件作品的交互性更强。但由于技术问题没有解决，所以没有做出来。我觉得这件作品还没有画上句号，延伸的空间还很多。

W&M　Are you satisfied with the final presentation of *The Sixth Channel*?

Ning　I initially wanted to create a frequency-modulated radio, where the content on the channels could be adjusted and DIYed by the audience, enhancing the interactivity of the artwork. However, due to unresolved technical issues, I couldn't implement it. I feel like this work hasn't reached its conclusion yet, and there's still a lot of room for further development.

未命名　**最后，我好奇的是，你会持续关注艺术介入现实之后所产生的影响吗？**

宁　我没有设想过我的作品会改变社区，我更希望看到的是，通过我的作品，观众获得了一种新的视角，他们在这个新的视角里看待社区的历史变迁。艺术不可能解决现实矛盾，但艺术介入的方式，可以让隐藏的社会问题暴露出来，从而找到更好的解决方案。艺术不是良方，而是药引，这是我喜欢公共艺术的原因。

W&M　Lastly, I'm curious, will you continue to monitor the impact generated by art intervention in reality?

Ning　I never envisioned that my work would change the community. What I hope to see is that through my work, the audience gains a new perspective, which allows them to view the historical changes of the community from this new viewpoint. Art cannot solve real contradictions, but the method of art intervention can expose hidden social issues, thereby finding better solutions. Art is not a cure but a prescription; that's why I like public art.

FM6.0 DAY1

20 世纪 80 年代，位于成都市玉林的一个小岛社区被称为青春岛，这是一个年轻人可以逃离城市生活压力，亲近自然的桃花源。

该岛位于岷江中游，只能乘船前往。周围是郁郁葱葱的绿色森林和波光粼粼的蓝色江水，岛上植被茂盛，可以探索的区域数不胜数。

青春岛的魅力就在于它可以让你将烦恼和焦虑抛在脑后，拥有使人能安静下来的力量，就像沙漠景观中的一抹绿洲。

来自各行各业的年轻人聚集在青春岛，共同的理想抱负和对冒险的渴望将他们紧密联系在一起。许多年轻人都会在夏天涌向这个岛，他们在丛林里搭起帐篷，在阳光下闲逛，在江水里游泳戏水。他们组成了紧密的社群，一起做饭，晚上围着篝火分享故事。在青春岛社区，人们可以放松警惕，找寻到本真的自己，他们可以逃离城市生活的压力，享受大自然的质朴。青春岛有着充满活力的文化场景，而文明诗歌是其创作精神的核心。诗歌朗诵，开放式麦克风和自发表演在青春岛是常见的景象，因此青春岛社区的空气中总是充满了抒情的，朝气蓬勃的声音的韵律。

自 2006 年以来，世界在许多方面发生了变化，因此青春岛并不总是平静和热情洋溢的。多年来，它经历了不少变化和动荡，但青春岛社区的精神依然存在。如今的青春岛已经不复往日，街道上空无一人，房屋也在分崩离析，但为数不多的住在这里的老人还记得岛上充满了青春的欢笑和喜悦。当我穿过青春岛安静的街道时，诡异的寂静充斥着整个社区，但后来我听到了一阵微弱的声音，就像鬼魂的窃窃私语。我停下来细细听，发现这是一个坐在破旧房子外面的老人吟诵诗歌的声音。

当我走近时，老人抬起头来，热情地笑了笑。欢迎来到青春岛。他说，我是梁柏，是这个社区的最后一位诗人。梁老先生邀请我坐下来，向我展示了他的一些诗歌，每一首诗都优美而令人难忘，唤起了对往昔青春岛居民充满激情和创造力的峥嵘岁月的追忆。梁老先生向我讲述了社区里挤满了艺术家，作家和音乐家的日子，他们来自中国各地，是青春岛充满活力和创意氛围的重要组成部分。就在梁老先生说话的时候，我几乎可以看到过去在我眼前鲜活起来。我想象着街道上挤满了人，空气中弥漫着音乐和笑声，青春岛的年轻人梦想着一个更美好的世界。

但后来，梁老先生的声音变得低沉起来，他告诉我青春岛的黑暗时期。青春岛社区因为一些社会事件的冲突而四分五裂，许多居民产生了意见和观念上的分歧，他们受到排挤和周遭的不理解，离开了青春岛，这个曾经充满活力的社区变成了一座鬼城，只剩下少数老人来纪念它过去的辉煌。梁老先生的诗歌捕捉到了青春岛的悲伤和失落，但也表达了希望和任性。他的话提醒我，即使在最黑暗的时代，仍然有美丽和力量有待发现。

当我离开青春岛时，我对这位与我分享他的故事的老人感到感激。他的诗歌让我想起了过去，让我看到了一个曾经因年轻人的活力和激情而蓬勃发

♫ 我走遍天涯路，用脚步留下铿锵的诗。
这里是 FM 第六故事频道，
每天下午 4：30 与您不见不散。

展的社区。当我离开的时候，我知道我会永远记住青春岛的美丽和韧性，以及让它保持活力的诗歌。

这些是我记下来的梁老先生的一些诗歌。

一

我在青春岛的中心地带，
火焰燃烧得明亮而真实。
对生活和美丽的热情，
这一点永远不会被压制。

二

青春岛的街道随着歌声回响，
年轻人和自由人的声音。
他们梦想着一个没有错误的世界。

三

在青春岛夜晚的黑暗中，
星光灿烂提醒我们，
即使在最黑暗的时代，
希望和美丽总是近在咫尺。

四

尽管世界可能会发生变化，
青春岛可能会逐渐消失，
它的精神将在诗歌中永存，
在那些留下来的人的心中。

THE VESSEL OF MEMORY

记 忆 的 容 器

未命名 **毕业到现在已经有一段时间了，你感觉有什么大的变化吗？**

杨懿 感觉思维变得比之前发散了。这几个月其实尝试了很多东西，没有完全局限在绘画创作上，我头一回参与了工作坊活动，也去尝试做了一些手工艺术品，比如“守护神”三代目、复刻我家猫面部的兽装，以及一些好玩的衍生品，我希望我的作品能被更多人喜欢。

W&M It's been a while since graduation. Do you feel any significant changes ?

Yang I feel that my thinking has become more divergent than before. In these months, I've tried many things, other than limiting myself to painting. For the first time, I participated in a workshop and also tried making some handicrafts, such as the "Guardian Spirit" third edition, an animal costume which replicates my cat's facial features, and some fun derivative products. I hope more people will like my works.

未命名 **这些面向大众的艺术衍生品里，有你想要表达的东西吗？**

杨 我当下的创作总是围绕一个核心的主题，生命与自然，它能激发我的创作欲，我也能在这个主题里找到乐趣。

我最近在做一个艺术衍生品，涉及到 TNR（Trap Neuter Release）的概念——一种以人道方式管理和减少流浪猫数量的方法，它的流程是诱捕、绝育、回置。城市里面有很多流浪猫，如果任由它们繁衍，流浪猫的数量会大幅增加，破坏当地的生态。一方面会给居民的生活带来不便，另一方面也会增加流浪猫的安全风险，比如说被投毒或被虐待。我做这些衍生品的目的是希望大众能了解这种观念，更好地保护流浪猫，这也是我的创作初心吧。

W&M In these art derivatives for the public, is there something you want to express?

Yang My current creations always revolve around a core theme—life and nature. It sparks my creative desire, and I find joy in this theme.

I'm currently working on an art derivative related to the concept of TNR (Trap Neuter Release)— a humane way to manage and reduce the number of stray cats. The process involves trapping, neutering, and returning. There are many stray cats inside the city, and if left unchecked, their population will increase significantly, disrupting the local ecosystem. On one hand, it inconveniences residents' lives, and on the other hand, it increases the safety risks for stray cats, such as being poisoned or abused. My goal in creating these products is to help the public understand this concept better and contribute to the protection of stray cats. This is also the initial intention behind my creations.

未命名　你是怎么找到“生命与自然”这个创作主题的？

杨　其实是一种本能的，抑制不住的喜爱。我看见这样的图像会很兴奋，很开心。

小时候，我迷恋上了一款游戏，《模拟动物人生》，它是一个多人在线游戏。如果我没有记错的话，它是在 2013 年 1 月 30 号左右在国内发布的。我一直玩了很多年，直到它停止运营。这款游戏就是让你去扮演动物并活下去，在自然环境里，需要去捕食，玩家之间有友情也有爱。我对创作动物形象的强烈动机最初来自于这个游戏。在玩这个游戏之前，小学四五年级的时候，我痴迷于阅读动物小说，比如沈石溪写的《狼王梦》《混血豺王》一类的。这是我童年乐趣所在。游戏和阅读体验中的动物，启发了我后来的创作。

W&M　How did you find the theme “life and nature” for your creative work?

Yang　It’s actually instinctual, an uncontrollable fondness. I get excited and happy when I see such images.

In my childhood, I became obsessed with a game, *Lif*, a multiplayer online game. If I remember correctly, it was released in China around January 30, 2013. I played it for many years until it ceased operations. This game allows you to play as an animal surviving in a natural environment, hunting for food, and experiencing friendship and love among players. My strong motivation to create animals initially came from this game. Before encountering this game, in the fourth and fifth grades of primary school, I was obsessed with reading animal novels, such as those written by Shen Shixi, like *The Dream of the Wolf King* and *Hybrid Jackal King*. These were the joy of my childhood. The animals in the game and the reading experience inspired my later creations.

未命名　兽装的制作会花掉你多少时间？

杨　一个月左右吧，但我做的时候也并不是朝九晚五的样子，中间会有一些空隙去调整，就像画画一样。画一阵子，就得停下来，退远看一下。如果一直闷头干，会困在局部里，容易出问题。节奏慢一点，中间会有一些时间反思，感受其他美的东西，这种状态对作品品质的控制会更好。

W&M　How much time does it take to make an animal costume?

Yang　About a month, but it’s not a nine-to-five job. There are breaks in between for adjustments to my work, just like painting, you need to stop for a while, step back, and take a look. If you keep working continuously, you might get stuck in the details and encounter issues. A slower pace allows time for reflection and appreciation of other beautiful things, which enhances the control over the quality of the work.

未命名 **你是用纯手工还是新的技术来创作的？**

杨 兽装的制作方法有好几种，在建模之前，我是用削海绵的方法，使用的材料是高密度海绵；或者用泥巴捏，然后倒模；还有一种方式比较现代，就是建模和 3D 打印。我一开始其实不想学软件，但当我削了一次海绵后就崩溃了，非常耗费体力和时间，学校也没有充足的空间，后来我就学习使用了 3D 建模和 3D 打印 。

W&M Did you use traditional handmade methods or new techniques for creation?

Yang There are several methods for making animal costumes. Before modeling, I used the method of cutting sponges, utilizing high-density sponge material. Alternatively, you can sculpt with clay and then make a mold, or use a more modern approach involving 3D modeling and 3D printing. Initially, I didn't want to learn how to use any software.But after cutting a sponge once, I was exhausted; it consumed a lot of energy and time, and the school didn't have sufficient space either. So later on, I learned how to use 3D modeling and 3D printing.

未命名　做兽装有一个填充的过程，从一张空白的布，最后变成一个立体的造型，与作画很相似。

杨　每一类艺术都是相通的。做兽装更像一个建造游戏：通过不断的搭建、组合各个部件的关系，去创造你想要的形象。绘画中的技法、色彩准确度、形体连贯性与整体节奏感，都会对制作兽装有帮助。

我毕业作品中的一个细节就是受到了兽装的启发。《房中天使》一开始没有加毛绒外框，放到展厅的时候，坚硬的木质外框总让我觉得缺少点什么。后来加上了白色毛绒，一切都变得柔软起来，它的质感像燃烧着的白色火焰。事后总结，原来这种触感，是我一直放不下的东西。

W&M　There is a process of filling content for making an animal costume, from a blank canvas to a three-dimensional shape, which is similar to painting.

Yang　Every form of art is interconnected. Making animal costumes is more like a building game: by continuously building and combining the relationships between different parts, you create the image you want. Techniques in painting, color accuracy, coherence of form, and overall rhythm will all be helpful in making animal costumes.

One detail in my graduation work was inspired by animal costumes. *Angel in the Room* did not have a plush frame at first. When it was placed in the exhibition hall, the hard wooden frame made me feel something was missing. Later, when I added the white plush to its frame, everything became softer, and its texture was like white burning flames. In hindsight, I concluded that this tactile sensation was something I couldn't let go of.

未命名　绘画和兽装似乎就是你创作天平的两端。

杨　目前是，小时候在家的乐趣不是画画就是做手工。童年喜欢做的事情，长大之后确也如此。

W&M　Painting and making animal costumes seem to be the two ends of your creative spectrum.

Yang　Currently, yes. When I was little, my joy at home was either painting or doing crafts. What I loved doing in my childhood has remained the same as I've grown up.

未命名 **今年毕业的学生的经历都很特殊，与往届的同学相比，你们没有太多机会在校园里生活、思考、创作、交流。所以我想知道居家学习的那段时间，你是怎么度过的？**

杨 刚上美院的时候，还没有多少自我探索，也经常会陷入到之前的创伤性回忆里，习惯从外界寻找认可，大多数时候都是琢磨怎样能够拿奖学金，如何成为被学校认可的优秀学生。也因为迎合标准，最后拿了一些奖项。

2020 年的时候，我回到广东，跟爸妈待在一起，养了一只猫，名叫“葡萄”。猫猫兽装这件作品其实就源于“葡萄”。

2021 年的时候，还在上网课，但我的身体出了问题，连着住了两次院。第二次医院都给了病重通知书。我离死亡很近了。我看着自己已经无法扎针输液的胳膊，听见病友痛苦的呻吟，我并不想就这么死，我一路熬过来，还什么都没做呢！生不足以成为动力的话，那死可以。

什么时候才开始干真正想干的事情呢？曾经设置的一层又一层必须满足的要求，意义是什么呢？被忽视的内心声音向我呼喊。为理想压抑了三年的热爱，必须得到释放。兽装是我内在精神的呈现方式之一。

早在 2016 年时，我就萌生了这个念头，那个时候信息没现在发达，制作更艰难。于是 15 岁的我只是在朋友圈等社交软件上感慨了一会儿，没有真正开始。2021 年我再次在微博感慨，这一次我得到了朋友的鼓励。出院之后，我开始行动了。

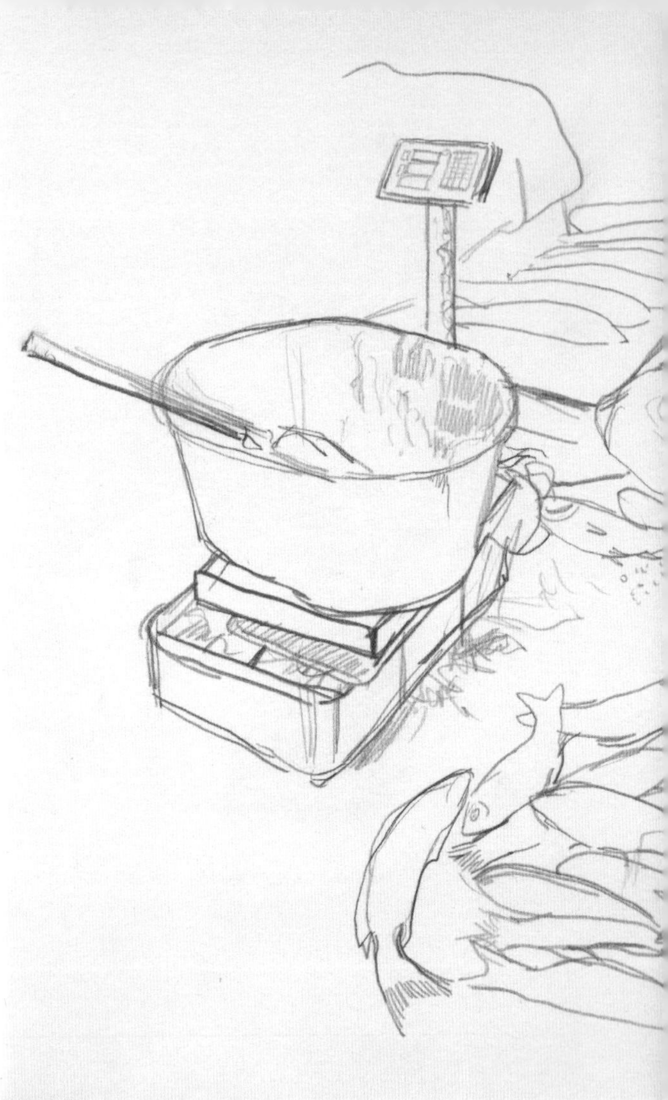

动物草图 II
Animal Sketch II

动物草图 I
Animal Sketch I

W&M This year's graduating students have had a unique experience. Compared to your seniors, you didn't have many chances to live on campus, or to think, create, and interact. So, I'd like to know how you spent the time studying at home?

Yang When I first entered the academy, there wasn't much self-exploration, and I often got stuck in past traumatic memories, seeking validation from the outside world. Most of the time, I was thinking about how to get scholarships and become an outstanding student recognized by the school. While conforming to standards, I ended up winning some awards.

In 2020, I returned to Guangdong, stayed with my parents and adopted a cat named "Putao". My cat costume work is actually inspired by "Putao".

In 2021, I was still taking classes online, but something went wrong with my health and I was hospitalised twice in a row. The second time the hospital announced I was critically ill. I was very close to death. I looked at my arm, which could no longer hold needles for fluids, and heard other patients moaning in pain; I didn't want to die just like that; I endured and survived all the way through. I have not done anything in my life yet. If life is not enough a motivation ,death is.

When did I start doing what I truly wanted to do? What is the meaning of the various requirements set in the past? The ignored inner voice was calling out to me. My passion suppressed for three years for the sake of ideals needed to be released. Animal costumes are one of the ways I express my inner spirit.

I had the idea back in 2016, when information wasn't as available as it is now, so creation was much more challenging. So, at the age of 15, I just expressed my feelings on social media for a while, without truly engaging. In 2021, when I expressed my feelings on Weibo again, this time, I received encouragement from friends. After being discharged from the hospital, I took action.

未命名 **那我们就过渡到毕业作品上吧。你的选题是怎么定下来的，中间都经过了哪些取舍？**

杨 我很渴望去创造一个能够让我有安全感的，或者说是能够满足我内心需要的一种空间。在那里，被更多的玩偶，更多的动物包围，能让我身心平静，感受到安抚和治愈。

为了画毕业创作，今年年初的前三个月，我留在了北京。我画的第一幅作品是《困兽犹斗》，我一直想画非常多的狼。如果不去画这张画，我可能会憋死的。后来终于画完了，我才稍微好受一些。之后和老师和同学们交流，感觉还可以再发散再扩展，就尝试画了各种各样的小稿。

热闹到极致的就是我要的安静，最后我的注意力就回到了我自己。

W&M Let's switch to your graduation work. How did you choose the topic, and what compromises did you make?

Yang I longed to create a space where I could feel safe, or a kind of space that would fulfill my inner needs. Being there, surrounded by more dolls, more animals, made me feel calm, soothed and healed.

To create my graduation work, I stayed in Beijing for the first three months this year. The first piece I painted was *Struggling Trapped Beasts*, as I always wanted to paint many wolves. If I didn't paint that, I might have suffocated. After finishing it, I felt a bit relieved. Later, after discussions with teachers and classmates, I felt there was room for expansion, so I tried painting various small drafts.

The ultimate bustle is the tranquility I desire, and, in the end, my attention returned to myself.

动物草图 III
Animal Sketch III

未命名 **为什么会选择狼的形象？**

杨 我从狼身上看到一种我需要的坚韧特质，是我渴望的珍贵品质。

W&M Why did you choose to paint the image of wolves?

Yang From the wolves, I see a tenacious quality that I need, a precious trait that I desire.

W&M In my view, wolves are always seeking their own pack. Like when we joke about someone being a "lone wolf", it means they have separated from the pack, placing themselves in the unknown. When I see the wolf in your work, there's a feeling that you also want to return to a certain community.

Yang I do like staying with companions, but I won't insist on relationships that have been destroyed. In my adolescence, I endured nearly half a year of being bullied on campus, and the pain of isolation is a vivid memory. The resilience and persistence of wolves can balance my mental stability.

Other creators might like horses or other animals. Maybe it's the elegance of horses or the inherent qualities of other animals that can bring some compensation to the soul and help people find a balance. This wolf pack, for me, is a kind of expansion of life.

The initial name of this painting was *Struggling*, later changed to *Struggling Trapped Beast*, but the meaning I wanted to convey was similar. I wanted to express the pain of the past in life, the struggle's agony that proves I once lived intensely.

As time passes, ordinary things are forgotten, and intense things are remembered. Later, I turned the wolf pack into a wolf skull and painted it in a self-portrait. I wanted it to be more in line with life, to be connected with things I usually encounter, not just lingering in the spiritual world.

未命名 **在我看来，狼始终在寻找自己的族群。比如我们开玩笑说一个人“独狼”，就说明它脱离了狼群，将自己置身于未知之中。当我在你的作品里看到它的时候，有一种感觉，似乎你也想回到某个集体里边。**

杨 我是挺喜欢和同伴待在一起，但已经毁灭的关系我并不会再强求。 在我青春期时，曾在校园里经历过大半年的校园霸凌，被孤立的痛苦是我真切活着的记忆。狼的坚韧与执着能够平衡我精神脆弱的部分。

其他创作者可能会喜欢马，或者别的动物。也许是马身上的优雅或者其他动物与生俱来的品性，能够给心灵带来一些弥补，帮助人们找到一种平衡。这群狼对我来说，是生命的一种扩张。

这幅画的名字一开始叫作《挣扎》，后面我又改成了《困兽犹斗》，但想表达的意思其实差不多。我想表达生命中的疼痛过往，这种挣扎的痛苦证明我曾经很强烈地活过。

随着时间的流逝，平淡的东西会被忘记，强烈的东西会让我记住。后来我把群狼变成一个狼头骨画在自画像里，我想要它更加契合生活，回到现实当中，跟我平时接触的事物发生关联，而不仅仅停留在精神世界。

自画像
Self-portrait

《困兽犹斗》
布面油画
120cm × 80cm
2023 年

Struggling Trapped Beast
Oil on Canvas
120cm×80cm
2023

杨　学院其实更希望作品去关注人，去描绘现实生活。完全依赖心灵感受和想象而创作的东西，由于缺乏经验和自我沉淀，容易有漂浮的感觉。为了避免这种情况的出现，应该找到情感的载体。我认可老师的说法，也从我的生活和感受里，找寻了可供我创作的元素。

在这之前，我还画了不少草稿。我本计划要画美院的草垛，它在美院的交叉路口，每天都会遇到。阳光照射在它那精修过的圆润的造型上，散发出一种很柔和的光色，很让我心动。在推进小稿的过程中，我察觉到自己无法很自然地向观众展示这是美院的草垛。而且也没有出现动物，让我很不痛快，后面就否定掉了。觉得毕业创作画草垛和我真正想要的表达的意味不太贴合。

否掉之后我又做了一些尝试，画了一只躺在地上的狗，画了老家广东珠海的一个地下商城，还去画了市场里的鱼，画了一个小男孩过马路……反正就是出了一些很生活化的稿子，当时觉得都没有那么贴切。到最后就憋得不行了，也不知道该从哪里下手。

画自画像最初是权宜之计，让自己不那么焦虑，顺便也找找感觉。我在自己面前放了一面镜子，画了一个正面像，我自然而然地在旁边画了一只没有肉身的漂浮着的狼头，有一种虚无感。周围还有一些花，以及我睡衣上的一些花纹。这张自画像是当时我认为最像我的一张。

画完这张画，我感觉是我想要的东西，后面就从自画像开始往下推。

我个人的视觉喜好是特别喜欢丰繁的图像，它能跟我的内心产生一些共鸣，让我觉得很愉悦。当时脑海中乍现了一个场景，我应该画一幅有我自己的画，这张画的构图是——我在中间，周围有非常多与我相关的东西，我被包裹着。有点喧闹，但是又透露着宁静，到处都是与我生命有关系的痕迹，我与它们相连。

接下来，我应该把自己置于什么样的场景之中?本来想画森林，后来感觉不够现实。我又想到了我的寝室。大一刚来美院宿舍的时候，我非常兴奋。寝室空间虽然不大，却让我十分依恋。那一小块区域是自由的，可以由我自己设计和装饰。很多时候，我在家里要听从父母的安排，而这个只属于我的宿舍空间让我很安心，让我找到了一个出口。

蜷缩在桌面中央的人物与我的一位室友有关。我的室友身形娇小，她自己买了一个小桌，放平常的桌面上，变成了桌中桌。装上帘子后，她坐在上面，变成了一个非常舒适的空间。

在小小的空间里蜷缩，能够给我一种很强的安全感。有一种自我保护，但又不是封闭的感觉。我也非常想那样干，但是我的体型比她庞大，于是我就想通过绘画实现我的愿望。(笑)

画中宿舍里的一些物件，它们都有我的生命痕迹。那只小黄鸭气球是我大一参加活动时留下来的，从 2019 年到现在，一直陪在我的身边。朋友们带回来的气球早都漏气了，可这只小黄鸭却很神奇保持着饱满状态。气球本身是脆弱的，但小黄鸭却一直鼓着气。我的内心也是脆弱的，但也在努力不泄气，我和它一样。

我把它安排在画面的上方，有一种上升的感觉。我想把它托起来，像托起我自己一样。

我还画了一本《了凡四训》，这本书背后就是我的成长经历。有些时候总感觉天都要塌下来了，有些困难好像无法克服，但最后都是通过相信和意念坚持下来了。念念不忘必有回响吧，后面我发现这句话好像是真的。你一直在想某件事情，无论如何也放不下，然后一直去做跟它相关的事情，总是会有一些回音出现。我在毕业创作里，也想表达相信的力量。

这幅画里我还放了另外一本书，《Great Women Artists》，书的封面 women 字符是被划掉的。我想通过这样的尝试，委婉地传达一下我相信的东西，也希望有人能够理解这种状态。

动物的元素是我一直放不下的。狼头骨出现在比较前方的位置，底下还垫了一本书，跟那个《Great Women Artists》也是有一点呼应，这本书是我非常喜欢的美国艺术家欧姬芙的一本自传。我很喜欢她的作品，她画很多花，也会画一些动物的头骨，她的画会给我一种很宁静舒适的感觉。作为一个女性艺术家，她极具开创性。

画面的左上角我画了一只正在向下伏击的豹子。“豹伏”的谐音是抱负。作品当中很多东西都是静态的，而豹子是动态的，静中有动。

其他一些小的元素包括漂浮的花朵，红色袜子，还有小火龙和守护神。那个小火龙其实也挺有意思，很多人看展就能够认出这种 IP 形象，我选择小火龙其实跟一些比较玄学的东西有关联。我有一个朋友很喜欢研究命理学，根据我的五行建议我在生活里可以多补充一些红色和黄色，状态会越来越好。我就买了一个小火龙，把它放在我的桌

《房中天使》手稿

The Sketch of *Angels in the Room*

GREAT
ARTISTS

上，像是一种默默无声的祈祷吧。透过不同的色彩，念念不忘，等待一个回响。

《守护神》是我结合了很多动物形体美感特征创作出的幻想生物。它是自然神的形象，一个再造的神明。“请虔诚地崇敬自然吧”，这是它所表达的。自然之力非常能疗愈我，所以我把它画在了小火龙的前面。

书架上还画了布洛芬，因为身体的原因，我经常会吃止痛药。身体的疼痛可以吃止痛药暂时缓解，但是心灵的伤痛又应该如何缓解呢，有没有一种药可以缓解内心的痛苦呢？我觉得还是得回到让自己安静下来的状态，回到房间，自己与自己对话，自己去疗愈心灵的伤口。

终于说到这幅画的名字，《房中天使》。它来自于一本女性主义著作《阁楼上的疯女人》，书中描绘的房中天使，是 19 世纪整天围绕着丈夫以及孩子团团转的女性，她们被比作天使，是完美的母亲和完美的妻子，但却没能成为自己，她们被这个角色牢牢地禁锢着，以一种不得已的方式变成“完美”的形象。我想通过我的作品去重新定义“房中天使”。

画面里的女性并不是完美的，她有自己的追求和渴望。她在思考如何成为真正的自己，而不是所期待的形象。有时候别人会问我，你把袜子画得这么艳干什么？袜子曾经是一块裹脚的布，它是历史上女性的一种遭遇。虽然今天这种束缚被抛弃了，但女性的生活中仍然有很多限制。

我已经对反自我反天性的“完美主义”追求有了抗拒，它对我的伤害并不小。

《房中天使》
布面丙烯
166cm×166cm
2023 年

Angels in the Room
Acrylic on Canvas
166cm×166cm
2023

①. 人与自然，，狗猫，
动物

草地上，倒影？

Yang My academy actually prefers works that focus on people and depict real life. Things created solely based on feelings and imagination can feel a bit floaty due to a lack of experience and self-reflection. To avoid that, it's important to find a vessel for emotions. I agree with my teacher and, from my own life and feelings, I also found elements I could use for my creations.

Before settling on my final graduation project, I went through several drafts. Initially, I planned to paint the grass mound at the intersection of the academy, a spot I encountered daily. The sunlight hitting on its well-manicured round shape, emitted a soft and pleasing glow that caught my attention. However, as I progressed with the drafts, I realized I couldn't naturally convey to the audience that it was the academy's grass mound. Plus, there were no animals, which made me uncomfortable. So, I scrapped that idea, feeling it didn't align with the deeper meaning I wanted for my graduation work.

After rejecting that, I tried various things: a dog lying on the ground, an underground mall in my hometown Zhuhai, fish in the market, a little boy crossing the road, and other mundane sketches. None of them felt quite right at the time. In the end, I was stuck and didn't know where to start.

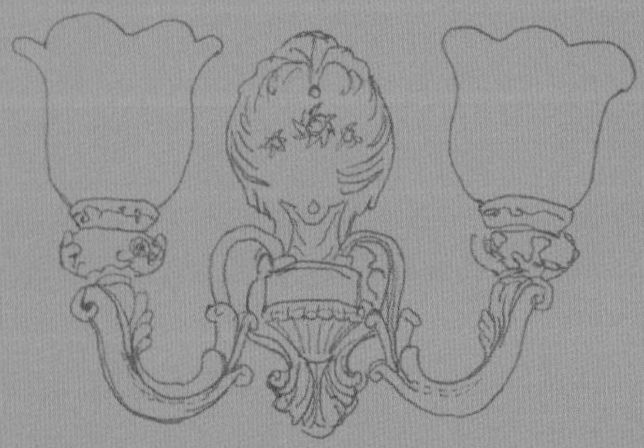

Creating a self-portrait was initially a makeshift solution to ease my anxiety and, at the same time, explore my feelings. I placed a mirror in front of me and drew a frontal image. Naturally, I added a disembodied wolf head floating next to me, creating a sense of emptiness. There were also some flowers around and patterns from my pajamas. At that time, I thought this self-portrait captured my likeness the best.

After finishing that painting, I felt it was what I wanted. From there, I started from the selfportrait and delved deeper.

My personal visual preference leans towards complex images that resonate with my inner self, bringing me joy. At that moment, a scene flashed in my mind: I should paint a picture with myself in it, where I'm in the center surrounded by numerous things related to me. It would be a bit chaotic but also exude tranquility, filled with traces connected to my life, intertwining myself with them.

Next, I had to decide what kind of scene I would like to set myself in. I initially thought of a forest but then felt it wasn't realistic enough. Then I thought of my dorm room. When I first came to the academy as a freshman, I was thrilled. Even though the dorm space wasn't large, I was very attached to it. That small area was free for me to design and decorate. I usually had to follow my parents' arrangements at home, but the space of my dorm was exclusively mine, which gave me peace and an outlet.

The figure curled up in the center of the desk is related to one of my roommates. She is petite and bought a small table, placing it on her usual desk, turning it into a sort of table on a table. With a curtain hanging, sitting on the top creates a very cozy space. Curling up in that small space gives me a strong sense of security. It's a form of self-protection, yet not a closed-off sensation. I really wanted to do that, but being larger in size, I decided to fulfill that desire through painting. Haha.

Some objects in the dorm, like the little yellow duck balloon, carry traces of my life. The balloon was from an event I participated in during my freshman year in 2019 and has stayed with me since. Other balloons from friends have long deflated, but this little yellow duck magically remains full. The balloon itself is fragile, but the little duck keeps itself inflated. My inner self is fragile too, but I'm also trying not to deflate, just like the duck. I placed it above in the painting, creating a sense of rising. I wanted to lift it up, much like lifting myself.

I also painted a book, *Liao Fan's Four Lessons*, which is the book behind my upbringing. There were times when I felt like the sky was falling, and some difficulties seemed insurmountable. Still, in the end, they were overcame through my belief and persistence. "If you think about something, it will eventually come back to you", and later on I realized that this saying seems to be true. If you keep thinking about something and can't let go of it no matter what, and then keep doing things related to it, there will always be some echoes sent back to you. In my graduation work, I also wanted to express this power of believing.

In this painting, I placed another book, Great Woman Artist, with the word "women" crossed out on the cover. Through this subtle attempt, I wanted to convey something I believe in and also hoped someone would understand this idea.

The element of animals is something I can't let go of. The wolf skull is positioned prominently upfront, with another book underneath, echoing the *Great Woman Artist*. This book is an autobiography of the American artist Georgia Totto O'Keeffe, whose work I really admire. She painted many flowers and some animal skulls, giving me a sense of tranquillity and comfort. As a female artist, she was highly pioneering.

In the top left corner of the painting, I depicted a leopard pouncing downward. The pun on "pouncing leopard" sounds like "aspiration" in Mandarin. Many elements in the work are static, but the leopard adds a dynamic element to it.

Some other small elements include floating flowers, red socks, the small fire dragon Charmander, and a guardian spirit. Charmander is interesting; many people recognize this IP character when they see it at our exhibition. My choice of this character is related to some mystical things. I have a friend who loves studying Chinese astrology. Based on my Five Elements, she suggested incorporating more red and yellow into my life for better well-being. So, I bought a Charmander toy, and placed it on my desk, like a silent prayer. It's like through different colors, constant remembrance, and waiting for an echo to be sent back to you.

The *Guardian Spirit* is a fantasy creature I created by combining aesthetic features of many animal forms. It represents the image of a nature deity, a reimagined divine being. "Please venerate nature sincerely" is its expression. Nature's power is incredibly healing for me, so I painted it in front of the small fire dragon Charmander.

I also painted ibuprofen on the bookshelf, because, due to health reasons, I often take painkillers. Physical pain can be temporarily relieved with painkillers, but how can the pain of the soul be alleviated? Is there a medicine to ease the inner pain? I believe it goes back to finding a quiet mind state, going back to my room, having a dialogue with myself, healing the wounds of my soul.

Finally, the name of this painting, *Angels in the Room*, comes from a feminist work called *The Madwoman in the Attic*. The angels in the room described in the book are women in the 19th century who revolved around their husbands and children all day, likened to angels—the perfect mothers and wives. Yet, they couldn't become themselves. They were firmly confined by this room angle role and, in a way, turned into this "perfect" image reluctantly. I want to redefine the "angels in the room" through my artwork.

The female figure in the painting is not perfect; she has her own pursuits and desires. She's contemplating how to become her true self, not the expected image. Sometimes people ask me, "Why did you paint the socks so vibrant?" Socks were once pieces of cloth used for binding feet, representing a historical experience of women. Although this form of restraint has been abandoned today, there are still many restrictions in women's lives.

I've developed resistance against the anti-self, anti-nature quest for "perfectionism". It used to cause quite a bit of harm to me.

未命名 **这种伤害具体是什么呢?**

杨 精神和身体上的创伤吧。失去自我，精神疼痛会变成瘤，变成癌。 就从画画来说，我认识到如果我没有发自真心去创作，就无法自我确认。当确认完全是由外界来主导，我的内心就会扭曲，会陷入无序的竞争和攀比中。

W&M What kind of harm are you specifically referring to?

Yang It's both mental and physical trauma. The mental pain of losing oneself turns into a tumor, and eventually becomes cancer. Speaking from the perspective of painting, I realized that if I don't create from my heart, I can't be self-affirmed. When confirmation is entirely dictated by the outside world, my inner self distorts and gets entangled in chaotic competition and comparison.

未命名 **你在用你的经验和创作去回应“房中天使”的比喻，而不是仅仅停留在思辨上。**

杨 我能做的就是把画画好，尽量的去做一些积极的回应。其实也没有想太多，这些东西正好在那时候显现，觉得能对得上，我就把它加进去，后面才逐渐找到一些线索，发现它们能彼此呼应。

W&M You're responding to the metaphor of "Angel in the Room" with your experiences and creations, not just dwelling on speculation.

Yang All I can do is paint as best as I can and try to make positive responses. Actually, I didn't think too much about it. Those things just emerged at some exact time, and they seemed fitting, so I incorporated them into the painting. Later on, I gradually found some clues and discovered that they could resonate with each other.

未命名 **一开始就只是日常经验中的物品，但是当你把它铺在画面上，这些符号似乎都有了意义，都与女性的某种自我探索产生了联系。**

杨 对，单个的物品对我的意义有限，但是把它们放在一起，意义就得到了延伸。创作过程当中，其实没有想太多，我就是去把自己生活里与我联系密切的东西，对我有意义的东西画进去，画着画着才发现它们形成了这种联系，产生了更深的理解。

W&M Initially, they were just everyday items, but when you lay them out on the canvas, these symbols seem to take on meaning, all connected to a certain self-exploration of females.

Yang Yes, for me the significance of individual items is limited, but when you put them together, the meaning extends. During the creative process, I didn't think too much. I just included things from my life that were closely related to me, things that had meaning for me. As I painted, I discovered that they formed this specific connection, which gave rise to my deepened understanding of those things.

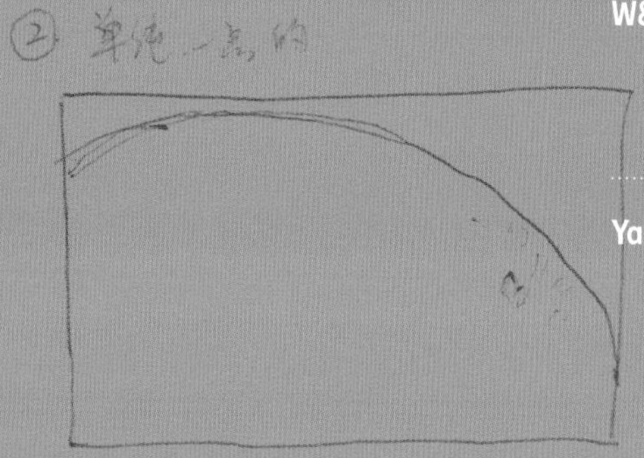

未命名　**《房中天使》画完后，你再给老师看，老师对你有什么回应吗？**

杨　老师们觉得这是我本科画的最好的一张。

W&M　After completing *Angel in the Room*, when you showed it to your teachers again, what was their response?

Yang　The teachers thought it was the best piece I painted during my undergraduate studies.

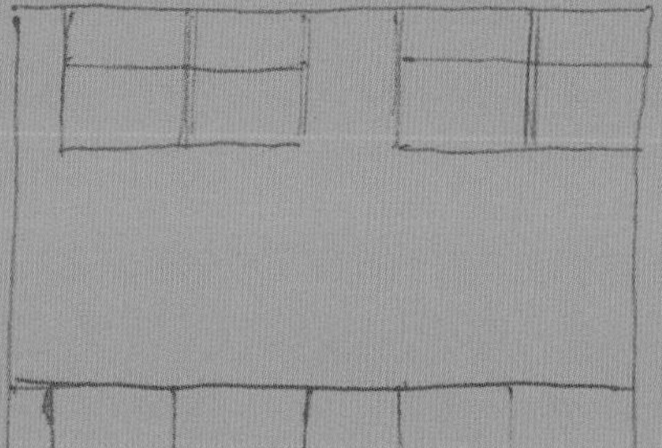

未命名　**另一幅《非劳心苦思，不能原事》里有怎样的故事呢？**

杨　这幅画是在《房中天使》之前完成的，在 2022 年 10 月份左右。那段时间，我每天往图书馆跑，看书学习让我找到了一种纯粹感，觉得内心精神有所丰盈。心境是比较静的，对世界也很敏感。

画中的男生其实是一个课程里的写生模特。我很早就来到画室，第一眼看到他的时候，就有一种说不出的难过。他是外来务工人员，来到北京打工，身上有一种漂泊无依令人心碎的感觉，一种无依无靠非常脆弱的生命状态。

这幅画的画框还是我捡来的，框上还刷了底。教室二楼的阁楼上，偶尔会有学长学姐废弃的画框。

W&M　What's the story behind another piece, *Without Laboring in Thought, One Cannot Grasp the Essence*?

Yang　This painting was completed before *Angel in the Room*, around October 2022. During that time, I went to the library every day. Reading and studying gave me a sense of purity, and spiritual fulfillment. My state of mind was relatively calm, and I was very sensitive to the world.

The guy in the painting is actually a live model from a class. I came to the studio very early, and when I first I saw him, I felt indescribably sad. He was a migrant worker who had come to Beijing for work, and there was a heartbreaking sense of drifting and vulnerability about him.

I actually picked the frame of this painting in the trash, and it was primed already. On the attic of the second floor of the classroom building, there are abandoned frames left by senior students occasionally.

未命名　这样的人物，是在你的绘画中第一次出现吗？

杨　我后来发现原来之前有过类似的。这个姿态在创作中反复出来了三次。在大二画的创作小稿里有个同样姿势的男人，旁边坐着一只像袋鼠一样的黄狗。

当《房中天使》和《非劳心苦思，不能原事》并置在一起，我发现原来我会本能地选择画蜷缩的姿态，也许跟我内心的不安全感有关系，以前还真没注意到。

画这个模特的那段时间，我还跟我的好朋友打过一个电话。她当时要画一朵百合花，问我应该怎么画。我对她说，其实对于百合花来说，你是当下唯一记录它的人。你对它竭尽全力，全神贯注，不管你画成什么样，这种真诚的记录已经足够了，除了你没有人会去在意这朵百合花。

当我看到模特的时候，我意识到，在那个时刻除了我没有人会在意他的脆弱和疲惫。我必须去记录下这种状态，把这种感觉留住。

作画的过程中，我对他形象做了一点轻微的变形，这也是我第一次感觉到所谓绘画当中的“变形”。在绘画里，人物也不一定非得就是模特原来的样子，我得把内心感受到的状态画出来。调整后的形象更像他，可能也更贴近于他的精神状态。

画面里还有一点小心思，但是注意的人很少。那个模特穿着一身黑，我在他的裤子边上画了一道红，又给他盖上一道黑色。其实是给他“穿”了一条红色的内裤，露出了小小的一角，算是我的一种祈祷。在中国人的传统里，流年不利的时候，有人会穿红色内裤。不管外部环境多么糟糕，人总是想做些努力，即使只是一种祈祷，说明他的精神还在挣扎。他脆弱的样子，感觉一拳就可以打倒，我给他加上的那抹红色，就是想给他在精神方面一些力量。

画完之后我还在想，要不再加点元素，加把伞或者什么的，但感觉怎么加都不对了。我之前画画有一个特点，同学也经常调侃我。工作室同学经常会这样说：“你！不要再画了！你再画就毁了！你现在已经很好了！”她们有时候会提醒我，那时候自己也意识不到。不过画《非劳心苦思，不能原事》，我恰好收住了。有时候我也在自我反思，这幅作品比我画《房中天使》要更加精炼一些，因为它是一口气完成的，从上午看到模特开始，我就再也没说过一句话，一直到画完，也没有跟朋友分享，久久地坐着，独自难过。

无题

Untitled

W&M Did this type of character appear in your paintings for the first time?

Yang I later discovered there were similar instances in my earlier paintings. This pose has recurred three times in my creations. In a sketch I did in my sophomore year, there was a man in a similar posture with a kangaroo-like yellow dog sitting beside him. When *Angel in the Room* and *Without Laboring in Thought, One Cannot Grasp the Essence* are placed side by side, I found that I instinctively chose to paint a curled-up posture. Perhaps it's related to my inner sense of insecurity, that's something I hadn't noticed before..

While painting this model, I also had a phone call with a close friend. She was trying to paint a lily and asked me how to do it. I told her that for a lily, she was the only one documenting its image at that specific moment. Wholeheartedly, with full concentration, regardless of how the painting turned out, the sincere documentation was sufficient. No one else would care about that lily at that time.

When I saw the model, I realized that at that moment, no one cared about his fragility and exhaustion except me. I had to capture his state at the moment, and preserve that feeling.

During the painting process, I made some slight deformations to his image. It was my first experience with what they call "deformation" in painting. In painting, characters don't necessarily have to resemble the model's physical appearance; I have to depict my internal feelings about the model. The adjusted image resemble him more closely, probably reflecting his mental state more accurately.

There's a subtle detail in the painting, but few people notice it. The model was dressed in all black, and I drew a red line on the edge of his pants, then covered it with black. In fact, I "gave" him a pair of red underwear, revealing a small corner. It's a sort of prayer for him from me. In Chinese tradition, some people wear red underwear during unlucky years. Regardless of how dire the external environment is, people always want to make some effort. Even if it's just symbolic, it shows that his soul is still struggling. His vulnerable appearance, as if he could be knocked down with a punch. But the touch of red I added is meant to give him some strength in his spirit.

After finishing the painting, I thought about adding more elements, like an umbrella or something else, but it just didn't feel right. I always had this tendency when painting, and my studio classmates often teased me about that. They would say, "Stop painting! You'll ruin it if you paint more! Your painting is already good enough!" Sometimes they would remind me when I couldn't realize it myself. However, with *Without Laboring in Thought, One Cannot Grasp the Essence*, I managed to stop at the right time. Sometimes, upon self-reflection, I feel this work is more refined than *Angel in the Room* because it was done in one go. From seeing the model in the morning to finishing the painting, I didn't say a word, nor did I share with my friends. I only sat there alone for a long time, feeling sad.

未命名 **这段话非常动人。**

杨 毕业创作时间跨度比较长，自己心里想的东西也多，这幅作品之所以我认为更加连贯，是因为我感觉我接住了那种情绪，从始至终都是一个念头。

W&M This is very soul-touching.

Yang My graduation project spanned a long period of time, and I had many thoughts in my mind. The reason why I consider this artwork to be more coherent is that I thought I captured that emotion within me, and it remained a consistent thought from beginning to end.

未命名 **这个作品应该给你带来了很多的可能，听说学校也收藏了，老师是怎么评价这个作品的？给你什么评语？**

杨 有哲思不可限量。

W&M This work must have opened up many possibilities for you. I heard your school also collected it. How did the teachers evaluate this work? What comments did they give you?

Yang Limitless philosophical thinking.

未命名　学校的评价让你有什么感受?

杨　我觉得挺感动的。触动自己真心的东西原来也能触动到他人。我觉得自己作品的数量还不是很多，经验也不够丰富，但外界给了我一个积极的反馈。告诉我可以按照自己的真心去做，可以成为想成为的自己。

之前听到一首歌，歌词里一个人跟一个机器人对话。那个人说："我真的可以成为自己想成为的人吗？"机器人说："当然可以，但是如果你这么想的话可能就不太行"。所以不要犹豫，直接去做就好。

回过头来，如果真心表达的东西，外界反馈还是很不好，那确实会很难过。明明好不容易才发的芽，庆幸的是，天哪，我没被踩死，甚至还有人给我浇了一点水，我很感动，太好了。

W&M　How did you feel about your school's evaluation?

Yang　I felt quite touched. It's surprising that something that genuinely moves me can also resonate with others. I don't have a large number of works, and my experience is not extensive, but the positive feedback from the outside world tells me I can follow my true feelings, and truly become the person I want to be.

I heard a song before with lyrics featuring a conversation between a person and a robot. The person asked, "Can I really become the person I want to be?" The robot said, "Of course, but if you think too much about it, it might not work." So, don't hesitate, just go and do it.

Looking back, if the things I express sincerely didn't get good feedback, it would indeed be upsetting. For my school's evaluation, it's like, "Finally, something's sprouting, and thank goodness, I wasn't stomped on! Someone even gave it a little water. I was deeply moved; it was great. "

未命名　获得这些认可之后，现在的你还会焦虑吗?

杨　稍微强了一点，但也还是有不安全感和焦虑的。

W&M　After receiving this recognition, do you still feel anxious now?

Yang　A bit less, but there's still that sense of not being completely secure and somewhat anxious.

《非劳心苦思，不能原事》
60cm × 80cm
布面丙烯
2023 年

Without Laboring in Thought, One
Cannot Grasp the Essence
60×80cm
Acrylic on Canvas
2023

未命名 **这个焦虑来自于哪里？**

杨 创作环境吧。比较明显的现象就是，我很少给自己认为“不够安全”的地方添置新家具。在学校的时候也有这样的感觉，工作室总会有外人进出，就不想在工作室买好一点的画架，以防受损，颜料柜也会本能性地买带锁的。那个地方让我不安，很多东西都被我收纳在寝室。虽然在寝室里我也放了一堆锁。

W&M Where's this anxiety coming from?

Yang The creative environment, I suppose. A clear example is that I rarely add new furniture to places I consider "not secure enough". I had a similar feeling back in school. Studios always have people coming and going; so I didn't want to invest in a better easel there to avoid it getting damaged. Even instinctively, I would buy a paint cabinet with a lock. That place made me uneasy, so I stored many things in my dorm. Even in my dorm, I also put locks on things.

未命名 **这与你的成长经历有关吗？**

杨 可能和陪伴有关吧。我一直都没法忘记一个场景，很小的时候，傍晚夕阳西下，我坐在沙发上，听到邻居家炒菜的声音，听到别的父母把小孩子叫回家的声音，我的爸爸妈妈却没回来，家里就只有我一个人。我坐在沙发上，看着夕阳落下，一直到天黑。过了很久，我才把灯打开，独自崩溃。说起来有点多愁善感，但确实难以忘怀。我的求学环境变动也很大，很早的时候就开始托管、住校，后面还去北京集训。周围的环境始终会让我紧张。所以我时常感觉自己需要锁和钥匙，或者尽可能不添置新东西。我觉得我守护不了的，就干脆不要拥有了。

W&M Does this tie back to your upbringing?

Yang Perhaps it's related to the idea of companionship. I can't forget a scene from when I was very young. In the evening, at the sunset, I sat on the sofa, hearing the sound of neighbors cooking, and other parents calling their children back home, but my parents hadn't returned, and I was alone at home. I sat on the sofa, watching the sunset until it got dark. After a long time, I turned on the light and broke down. It may sound sentimental, but it's indeed unforgettable. My educational environment changed a lot, too. I started boarding and living at school very early, and later, I went to Beijing for training. The changing environment around me always makes me nervous. So, I often feel like I need locks and keys, or I try not to acquire new things. If I feel I can't protect it, I'd rather not have it.

未命名 **但是你似乎想把这些东西都藏在画面里边。**

杨 因为我想让这幅画有纪念性。可能这些东西后来都不在了，但那张画还在。

我小的时候，表妹来家里玩，我送了她很多娃娃，但在送之前，我把每个娃娃都画了下来，最后把娃娃给她，我留下的是画纸上的娃娃。

W&M But it seems like you want to hide all these things in your paintings.

Yang Because I want this painting to be a keepsake. Maybe these things won't remain later, but that painting still exists.

When I was young, my cousin came to play at my house. I gave her many dolls, but before giving them away, I drew each doll. In the end, I gave her the dolls, and I kept the drawings.

未命名 **之前的创作里有这种心理动机吗？**

杨 之前没有想过用这种方式创作，只是后来临近毕业，那些东西都要带走。那段时间我很焦虑，不知道我的东西应该去往何方，寄回家也很奇怪，好像在北京认真求学了几年之后，一夜之间打回原形。当时我想尽了各种办法把能够清理的东西转卖掉。最后马上要毕业了，我突然开始装饰我的工作室。临近离开了，就控制不住地想干点匪夷所思的事。现在看其实像是一种纪念碑式的依恋。

W&M Was this psychological motivation present in your earlier works?

Yang I never thought about creating in this way before. It only came to me near graduation when those things had to be taken away. I was very anxious during that time, not knowing where my things should go. Sending them back home was strange. It felt like, after diligently studying in Beijing for several years, I suddenly reverted overnight. At that time, I tried various methods to sell the things I could clear out. Finally, as graduation approached, I started decorating my studio. Approaching departure, I couldn't control the urge to do something bizarre. Looking back now, it's actually like a monumental attachment to my belongings.

未命名　现在的创作应该能够支撑你的生活开销吧。

杨　目前还不算能完全支撑，大部分时候还是在各种尝试探索。有趣的是，消费观念这一年也有改观，不再按照冲动欲望去消费，反而更在意防御力。

W&M　Your current work should be able to support your living expenses, right?

Yang　Not quite able to fully support me at the moment. Most of the time, I'm still trying to explore various possibilities. What's interesting is that my perspective on consumption has also changed this year. I no longer consume based on the impulsive desire to spend, but am more concerned about the defences in the face of life.

未命名　这跟父母有关吗?

杨　没有，就只是跟自己的一些阅读和接触到的人与事有关系，更加在意防御力而不是攻击性，不会为了一时新鲜作出冲动的决定。为了走得更远，更长久。

我感觉自己有点像只乌鸦，非常喜欢华丽的亮闪闪的泛着光泽的东西。大一的时候很喜欢穿的金光闪闪，毛茸茸。不过随着成长，要考虑的东西在增加。善守者，藏于九地之下；善攻者，动于九天之上。

W&M　Is this related to your parents?

Yang　No, it's just related to some of my own readings, and people and events I encountered. I care more about defense rather than aggression, avoiding impulsive decisions for momentary freshness. It's about making efforts for a longer-lasting and far-reaching goal.

I feel a bit like a raven, very much a fan of gorgeous, shiny, and glossy things. My freshman year was very much about wearing bling and fluff. But as I grew up, there were more things to consider. As the old saying goes, "The adept takes refuge deep underground, the skilled attacker moves high above the sky."

未命名　艺术家得有自己的生存之道。

杨　中国骂人有句话，“不得好死”。（笑）考虑到如何“好死”，人就得提前打算。

无聊的时候我就想，我以后究竟以什么样的方式离开这个世界。我幻想着，我应该在一个很明媚的午后，晒着温暖的阳光，周围环境都很好，我的理想完成了，财产分配好了，子女也安顿好了，我在花园躺椅安然小憩，不再醒来。

W&M　Yeah, artists need to have their own way of survival.

Yang　In China, there's a phrase used as an insult, "may you die a bad death" ha-ha. Considering how to "die well", one has to plan ahead.

When I'm bored, I sometimes think about how I'll leave this world in the future. I fantasize that I should leave on a bright afternoon, basking in warm sunlight, with a pleasant environment, my ideals fulfilled, assets allocated, children settled, and I'm peacefully napping on a garden lounge chair, never to wake up again.

PURE

纯粹的愉悦

JOY

陈晓奎：我成长在上海，祖籍是广东潮州，我的父母都会画画，小时候当我静不下来时，妈妈就会给我纸笔。选择绘画，的确受了家里影响，但更多还是自己喜欢。

到了毕业的时候，除了画画还要准备考研，所以给我准备毕设的时间并不多。但毕设又是如此之重要，就有些过分上心了。我的母亲当时还查出了甲状腺癌。

Chen Xiaokui: I grew up in Shanghai, but my ancestry traces back to Chaozhou in Guangdong. Both my parents knew how to draw, and when I was little, my mother would hand me paper and pens when I couldn't sit still. My choice of painting was indeed influenced by my family, but on top of that, I loved it.

When I was about to graduate, I had to juggle painting and preparing for the postgraduate entrance exam, so I didn't have much time to prepare for my graduation project. But the project was so crucial, and I became overly concerned about it. At the same time, my mother was also diagnosed with thyroid cancer.

未命名　她现在病情好点了吗?

陈　好一些，甲状腺癌在癌症里面是最懒的癌，不容易扩散。当时我之所以那么担心，是因为她从健康的状态，变得非常嗜睡，非常怕冷。当我跟爸爸都感觉不到冷的时候，她需要裹很多的衣服，我觉得她好像马上要离我而去。

我跟母亲一直都有很深入的交流，是她一直带着我画画。她牺牲了自己的事业，做了全职的家庭主妇，一直陪着我学，从小陪到现在。那一段时间，我其实特别紧张。除了考试，我非常害怕失去母亲。她是唯一能跟我的灵魂沟通的人。仅仅一个眼神，她也能知道我心中所想。所以我特别想通过绘画表达我心里的感受，以及对她的感情。

初稿画出来的时候，老师告诉我:“晓奎，我觉得你不够放松。”我意识到它只是图像的拼凑，于是开始试着感受什么是放松。后来我去了一直想去的北京海洋馆，回来以后就开始画各种小鱼、鲸鱼。

但那次经历并没有让我放松，相反还挺难受的。海洋馆里有个很短的海底隧道，我路过拍照时，突然就有一条蝠鲼游过来，它的翅膀划过水面，我觉得自己好幸运，居然能在那么短的海底隧道拍到它。后来我坐在水族箱前面观察，发现大部分鱼游的都是一样的路径，像机器一样，唯一有所改变的是那群小鱼，那一刻真的挺难受的。

我画了一组鱼，颜色非常艳丽，就像在霓虹灯下穿梭。但是当时给妈妈看了以后，她感觉这些鱼好拘谨啊。她确实太了解我了!

我犹豫过要不要画母亲这个题材，担心是不是太刻意了。有一天终于想通了，既然要画得放松，那就去把布买回来，想画什么就画什么。

这次创作我做过方法上的调整，之前的作品在表达情感时，总是事先设想一个故事或场景。现在我只想表达一个词，就是失去或者重生。当我只关注情感本身的时候，画布上所呈现的东西，就都由我自己掌控，一切都轻松起来，一切都纯粹起来。

W&M　Is she feeling better now?

Chen　Yeah, somewhat better. Thyroid cancer is considered one of the less aggressive forms of cancer and does not spread easily. But I was so worried at that time because she went from being healthy to being very lethargic and very sensitive to cold. When my father and I felt fine in our regular clothing, she needed to wrap herself in layers, making me feel like she might slip away from me at any moment.

My mother and I have always had a very deep connection, and she was the one who always guided me in painting. She sacrificed her career, became a full-time housewife, and has accompanied me in learning painting from my childhood until now. At that time, I was actually very on edge. Apart from exams, I was scared of losing my mother. She was the only person who could understand my soul. With only a glance, she could get what I'm thinking. So I especially wanted to pour my heartfelt feelings and emotions for her through my paintings.

When my initial draft came out, my teacher told me, “Xiao Kui, I feel you are not relaxed enough.” I realized the draft was just a composition of images, so I started trying to feel what it means to relax. Later, I went to the Beijing Aquarium, which I had always wanted to go to, and when I came back I started drawing all kinds of small fish and whales.

But that experience didn't make me relax, instead, it was quite uncomfortable. There was a very short underwater tunnel in the aquarium, and as I passed through to take photos, suddenly a batfish swam by, its wings cutting through the water, and I felt so lucky to capture it in such a tiny tunnel. Later as I sat in front of the aquarium observing the fish, I noticed most of them just swam the same path, like machines, with the only exception being a group of small fish. It was a truly unsettling moment.

I painted a group of fish with super bright colors, like they were swimming through neon lights. However, when I showed it to my mother, she felt that the fish were so restrained. She does know me well!

I thought a lot about whether to paint my mother as the subject, worried it might seem too deliberate. One day, I finally figured out that if I wanted to paint in a relaxed manner, I should just go and grab a canvas and paint whatever came to my mind.

This time, I made some adjustments to my painting approach. In previous works, I always preconceived a story or scene in advance when expressing my emotions. Now, I only want to express a single word—loss or rebirth. When I focus solely on the emotion itself, everything on the canvas becomes under my control, everything is relaxed, everything is pure.

《爱是一场与时间的赛跑》
布面油画
200cm×150cm
2023 年

Love is a Race Against Time
Oil on Canvas
200×150cm
2023

未命名 **也许人只有遭遇过紧张，才会有机会变得轻松吧！你的作品表达出了一种真正的取舍。**

陈 大三的时候，我画过家里的猫。对我而言，这件作品是把记忆留下来，并不是对某个时刻的写实记录。它在技法上是自由的，使用了点彩的画法，但还不够成熟。到了毕业创作的阶段，我会更自觉地通过绘画来表达我的记忆和感受。

W&M Perhaps, only after experiencing tension can one truly find relaxation! Your artwork conveys a genuine sense of choices.

Chen During my junior year, I painted my family cat. For me, that work was about preserving memories rather than creating a realistic depiction of a specific moment. Technically, it was pretty loose, using a pointillism technique, but it wasn't mature enough. As I approached my graduation projects, I was more conscious about using painting to express my memories and feelings..

未命名 **我第一次看到《爱是一场与时间的赛跑》，有一种非常强烈的感受——神圣性，画面中人物的面庞既像天使，又像是死神。不过这只是我自己的感受，也许不是你想要表达的。**

陈 当时的创作发生过很巧合的事情，第一次画的时候，油给的比较多，画布会形成反光。第二次再去刻画脸，用的油没那么多，形成了哑光的效果。最后装裱的时候，我无意间发现人物的脸上有骷髅的形状。这是关于我妈妈的一张画，当我看见骷髅的时候，我知道她会早一步离开我，所以心情并没有崩溃，我只想在剩下的时间里去做些什么。

W&M The first time I saw *Love is a Race Against Time*, I had a very intense feeling—a sense of sacredness. The faces of the characters in the painting seemed like angels and, at the same time, like the grim reaper. But maybe that's just my own interpretation, not necessarily what you intended to express.

Chen There was a coincidence during the creation of that piece. The first time I painted it, there was a bit too much oil, causing a reflective effect on the canvas. When I went back to work on the faces the second time, I used less oil, creating a matte effect. It was only during the framing process that I unintentionally noticed a skull shape on the character's face. This painting is about my mother, and when I saw the skull, I knew she would leave me sooner. So, I didn't break down emotionally; I just wanted to do something with the time that remained.

未命名 **从你的习作到毕业创作，似乎能够看到你内心对于神圣性的不自觉的探索。**

陈 可能跟小时候的经历有关，我爸爸是一个非常喜欢古典的人，会买很多画册，小时候在家翻的都是文艺复兴时期的画，很多都跟宗教有关。就像一杯水在某一个阶段倒进了一种液体，之后就很难分离出来了。

W&M From your early works to your graduation project, it seems like an unconscious exploration of the sacred within you...

Chen It might be related to my childhood experiences. My dad is really into classical stuff and used to buy a lot of art books. I grew up flipping through books about Renaissance paintings, many of which were related to religion. It's like pouring a liquid into a cup of water at a certain stage; afterward, it's nearly impossible to separate.

未命名 **在那个阶段，艺术对你而言似乎有了一种疗愈的作用。**

陈 是这样。

W&M During that period, it seems like art had a healing effect on you.

Chen Yes, it did.

《纱帘后 · 二》
布面油画
87.5cm×55cm
2023 年

Behind the Veil II
Oil on Canvas
87.5×55cm
2023

未命名　后来你有试着重新思考过这段经历吗?

陈　有过，我跟母亲讨论过这件事。身边的同学性格各异，有的想出名，有的想在绘画艺术上有所成就。我觉得大家的理想都很丰满，很欣赏他们，而我只想把我的感受画出来。这一点跟我的母亲有关，她是一个内求的人。

W&M　Have you ever tried to reconsider this experience later on?

Chen　I have. I discussed it with my mother. My classmates around me had diverse personalities—some wanted fame, some aimed for success in painting and art. I admired their lofty ideals, but I just wanted to express my feelings. This has to do with my mother; she's an introverted person.

未命名　她的思维方式影响了你。

陈　对，没错。

W&M　Her way of thinking influenced you.

Chen　Exactly.

未命名　绘画需要专注，向内求或许就能提供源源不断的动力。

陈　没错，当你坚定下来要寻找某个东西，真的会不顾一切，我挺享受这其中的过程。人在全身心投入的时候会进入一种心流的状态，我感受到自己与整个世界连在一起。

W&M　Painting requires focus. Perhaps seeking inwardly can provide a continuous source of motivation.

Chen　Absolutely. When you're determined to find something, you'll go all out for it. I really enjoy the process. When you're fully immersed, you enter a state of flow, feeling connected to the entire world.

《On My Way》
布面油画
50cm×160cm
2023 年

On My Way
Oil on Canvas
50cm×160cm
2023

未命名　在绘画之外，你是怎么感受这个世界的呢?

陈　课余时间我们有一个穿行社，会跟学校里面的朋友去爬山、徒步，我是很喜欢爬山。

W&M　Apart from painting, how do you experience the world?

Chen　In my free time, I'm part of a hiking club. We go mountain climbing and hiking with friends from school. I really enjoy hiking.

未命名　你的绘画里似乎还没有出现过风景的元素。

陈　徒步爬山，对我来说是一种修行，暂时没有想要把它变成绘画的题材。现在这个阶段，我想探求的是人的情绪本身，正面的或负面的。我的好朋友推荐我阅读一本书，赫尔曼·黑塞的《悉达多》，对我启发非常大。这本书与佛教有关，影响了我理解这个世界的方式。用黑塞的语气来说，当你要去感受艺术时，你也就感受到了世界。我最近创作的新的系列绘画《何以为我》，就是在寻找，真正的我究竟是什么样的。我想去理解和接纳这些多样的情绪。

W&M　It seems like elements of landscapes haven't appeared in your paintings yet.

Chen　Hiking and mountain climbing are forms of spiritual practice for me. For now, I haven't thought about turning it into a painting theme. At this stage, I want to explore human emotions, whether positive or negative. A good friend recommended a book to me, Hermann Hesse's *Siddhartha*, which has greatly inspired me. The book is related to Buddhism and has influenced my understanding of the world. In Hesse's words, when you experience art, you're also experiencing the world. The new painting series I've been working on recently, *What is Me*, is about seeking, trying to understand what my true self is like. I want to comprehend and accept these diverse emotions.

《月泉》
布面油画
150 cm×120cm
2023 年

Moon Spring
Oil on Canvas
150cm×120cm
2023

未命名 **在创作的过程中，你会把“情绪”放在艺术史的维度上来考察吗?**

陈 嗯，目前还没有。

W&M During your creative process, do you examine "emotion" within the context of art history?

Chen Hmm, not currently.

未命名 **可能是我的问题预设了一个学术立场，而你作画的方式完全来自于个体的经验。**

陈 能理解您的问题。绘画有时候是自我的观察，但不是以自我为中心。不过，相比我的朋友我可能确实欠缺这个领域的知识（笑）。

W&M Perhaps my question assumed an academic standpoint, and your approach to painting comes entirely from personal experience.

Chen I understand your question. For me, sometimes painting is a self-observation without selfcentering. However, compared to my friends, I may indeed lack knowledge in this field, haha.

未命名 **那我们回到作品上，为了创作你会特意观察母亲的生活习惯吗?**

陈 会（笑）。小时候没有观察过她，可能会有这样一种心理，我是你的孩子，你照顾我是应该的，长大以后就不会了。有一次，我打开衣柜，发现了里边的灰尘。我问妈妈，为什么我的衣柜每天都关着还会有灰尘？妈妈回应我说，干净是人创造出来的环境。我那会儿才意识到，原来是她一直在为我所生活的环境付出。如果有一天，我做了母亲，会不会像她一样有耐心。观察她的时候才发现，她是我的一个榜样。

W&M Let's go back to your works. Do you consciously observe your mother's daily habits in order to create your works?

Chen Yes, ha-ha. I didn't observe her when I was young, I might have the mentality that I was your child and taking care of me was what you should do, but not when I got older. Once, I opened my wardrobe and found dust inside. I asked my mother why my wardrobe was still dusty even though it was closed every day. Mum responded to me by saying that cleanliness is an environment created by people. I realised at that moment that she had been the one who had been creating the environment I lived in. If I become a mother one day, will I be as patient as she is? It was only when I observed her that I realised she was a role model for me.

《静谧空间》
木板油画
30cm×50cm
2023 年

Tranquil Space
Oil on Wood Panel
30cm×50cm
2023

未命名 **衣柜里的灰特别有意思。从前的我们可能默认所有东西都应该是光亮如新，突然间发现原来这个地方曾经是有过灰的，只不过擦过灰的那个人我一直没有观察到。就像薛定谔的猫一样，你观察到它的时候，它可能就改变了。**

陈 是这样的。

W&M The dust in the wardrobe is quite interesting. Once upon a time we might have tended to the idea that everything should be shiny and new, and then suddenly we realise that the place was once dusty, only that the person who wiped it down was someone I hadn't been observing. Like Schrodinger's cat, it may have changed by the time you observed it.

Chen Exactly.

《暖》
布面油画
87.5cm×55cm
2023 年

Warmth
Oil on Canvas
87.5cm×55cm
2023

《粉红绒》
布面油画
129cm×200cm
2022 年

Pink Velvet
Oil on Canvas
129cm×200cm
2022

《祈》　布面油画　100cm×160cm　2020 年

Pray　Oil on Canvas　100×160cm　2020

未命名　你的绘画语言经历过什么样的变化？

陈　我很喜欢古斯塔夫·克里姆特的绘画，在画《纱帘后》时，曾经尝试过他那标志性的圆圈，画上去之后，我立马就擦掉了，原因是非常不和谐。我后来总结，克里姆特的绘画语言是从他自身的生命体验中提炼出来的，而我只是喜欢他的作品，并不能成为他。在这之前，我其实一直在提高技法，探索色彩，缺乏对生活的观察。我的老师对那个时候的我也并不满意，觉得我对色彩的理解是概念化的，她更希望我去关注现实，现实里的颜色往往更漂亮。

《月泉》与《爱是一场与时间的赛跑》是同一时期的作品，我经常画着画着就开始哭，因为时间在跑，不会停下来，妈妈的病情当时也没有出现好转。春天的一个午后，我路过学校的一个花坛，看见了一片黄绿色的小草，刚刚浇完水。在此之前，我从未感受到如此强烈的生机，它的颜色一下子刺激到了我。然后我打起精神，自我鼓励，可是我妈妈没走啊，那么伤心干什么呢？我还能陪她很久，为什么要想这么糟的事儿！

一开始创作的时候，我没有想到要画哺乳的婴儿，只是想把那些颜色表达出来，把生机感画出来。我去创作它，也没想过参加展览，为的是让我心情好起来。最后以哺乳的形式呈现出来，完全是一种巧合。

W&M　How has your painting language evolved?

Chen　I really like Gustav Klimt's paintings. When I painted Behind the Veil, I tried his iconic circles on my painting. After putting them on, I immediately wiped them off because they were very disharmonious. Later, I concluded that Klimt's artistic language is distilled from his own life experiences, and I just like his works, I can't become him. Before this, I was focused on improving painting techniques, exploring colors, but lacked observation of life. My teacher was not satisfied with me at that time, thinking my understanding of color was conceptual. She wanted me to focus on reality; colors in reality are often more beautiful.

Moon Spring and *Love is a Race Against Time* are works from the same period. I often started to cry while painting because time was slipping away, and my mother's condition wasn't improving. One afternoon in spring, I was walking past a flowerbed in my school and saw a patch of yellowgreen grass that had just been watered. Before that, I had never felt such a strong sense of life, its color stimulated me at once. Then, I cheered up and encouraged myself: mom hadn't left yet, so what was the point of being so sad? I could still be with her for a long time. Why think about such depressing things!

Initially, when creating that work, I didn't intend to paint a breastfeeding baby. I just wanted to express those colors and vitality. I didn't think about participating in an exhibition; I just wanted to lift my spirits. The breastfeeding form emerged as a complete coincidence.

未命名 **《月泉》的视觉效果还像海洋里向上生长的水草，想要捕捉阳光，有一种流动感。**

陈 您这个看法跟我妈妈一样，她觉得也是像水里面的水草，摇曳着吸收阳光。刚开始画，是一株株草，有根茎，有分叉。画到后面，它与乳腺的形状越来越像。从身体里面汇聚出来的乳汁，养育下一代。这幅画算是随着性子走，也有一定的巧合性。

W&M The visual effect of Moon Spring also resembles aquatic plants growing upward in the ocean, trying to capture the sunlight, creating a sense of flow.

Chen Your viewpoint is the same as my mom's, and she thinks it also looks like underwater plants swaying to absorb sunlight. At the beginning, I painted individual grass stems with roots and branches. As I progressed, it started resembling the shape of a mammary gland. Milk gathers from the inside of the body, nurtures the next generation. The painting sort of evolved with my nature, and there was also a certain element of coincidence.

《情绪系列 · 妒》
布面油画
60cm×180cm
2023 年

Emotion Series: Envy
Oil on Canvas
60cm×180cm
2023

未命名　婴儿是最后画的吗？

陈　第一遍就有。婴儿和母亲的手全都是第一遍画的。我当时画完旁边的绿色，就特别想让中间出现黄色色块，但我不想让它是其它形状。我更喜欢球体，它更舒缓一点，再加上我很喜欢蓝绿色，所以后来又加了一点蓝绿色上去。婴儿的额头、鼻子和嘴其实都是随机形成的，有种波洛克的感觉，甩出来的。

W&M　Is the baby the last thing you painted?

Chen　It was done in the first attempt. The baby and the mother's hands were all painted in the first try. After finishing the green on the side, I particularly wanted to introduce a yellow block in the middle, but I didn't want it to be a different shape. I preferred a sphere, which is more soothing. Plus, I really like turquoise, so I added a bit of turquoise later. The baby's forehead, nose, and mouth were randomly formed, giving a Jackson Pollock feel, splattered.

未命名　画完毕业作品，你的老师有什么评价？

陈　她非常喜欢《爱是一场与时间的赛跑》，她认为我通过这件作品算是初窥门径，找到了创作的路，对我的进步比较欣慰。她也是做母亲的，也有一个女儿。她们之间的感情，我并不了解。但是我母亲和我的导师在看这幅画的眼神是一样的，希望我没有揣测错。

W&M　After completing your graduation work, what feedback did your teacher give?

Chen　She really liked *Love is a Race Against Time*. She thought that through this work, I had taken the first step and found the path of creation, and she was pleased with my progress. She is also a mother and has a daughter. I don't know much about their relationship, but my mother and my supervisor had the same look in their eyes when they looked at this painting. I hope I didn't misunderstand it.

未命名　你有思考过女性画家的身份，或者状态吗？

陈　有考虑过，我的一个朋友，她画的是女生宿舍，颜色非常鲜亮。当时我问她那个窗为什么是红的，是血月来了吗？她回答说，其实作为女性的我们都能感觉到，外面的社会可能有危机存在。我们之间讨论过女性画家在这个时代的地位，我的看法是，我更想画好我想画的东西，如果我的画有幸能为女性画家发声，能够帮到她们，我会很开心，哪怕能帮到男性画家我也很开心。目前唯一能够做到的，就是好好表达我自己。

W&M　Have you ever thought about the identity or position of being a female artist?

Chen　I have considered it. One of my friends paints scenes from a girls' dormitory with very bright colors. I asked her why the window was red, was it a blood moon? She replied that, as women, we can all feel that there may be a crisis in the outside world. We have discussed the position of female artists in this era. My view is that I would rather paint what I want to paint. If my paintings can voice female artists and help them, I would be happy—even if it helps male artists, I would still be happy. Currently, the only thing I can do is express myself sincerely.

未命名 **你的作品从伦理情感上表达了两个女性之间的联系。**

陈 我很想多维度地表达跟母亲之间的关联，不是简单的爱意传递。但当时的我没有能力表达出来，因为它是一个抽象的东西。情绪或情感不是故事，而是自己的感受。从毕业到现在，我仍然在思考着这个主题。我想把我的感受画出来，也许观众可能没有理解，但我画了一张令我满意的画，我会非常非常的开心。我宁愿画自己喜欢的，有人可能不喜欢，但至少我真诚地表达了自己，没有违背我的内心，活着本身就已经要干很多违背自己的事情了。我已经尝到过画自己喜欢的画所带来的快乐，它让我觉得原来活着如此美好，让我想去感受，让我想要认真地活着。

W&M Your work expresses the emotional connection between two women from an ethical standpoint.

Chen I really want to express the connection with my mother in multiple dimensions, not just a simple conveyance of love. However, at that time, I was not capable of expressing it because it was an abstract thing. Emotions or feelings are not stories but what one feels. From my graduation until now, I am still thinking about this theme. I want to paint what I feel, maybe the viewer may not understand it, but I will be extremely happy when I paint a picture that satisfies me. I prefer to paint what I like; some people may not like it, but at least I express myself sincerely, not going against my heart, and living itself already involves doing a lot of things against myself. I've already tasted the happiness that comes from painting what I like, it makes me feel so good to be alive, it makes me want to feel, it makes me want to live earnestly.

未命名 **你的自我认同完全与你的创作是一致的。**

陈 我始终都在回想我小时候画画的状态，那种开心的感觉真的是没有什么能够比拟的。

W&M Your self-identity is completely in line with your creations.

Chen I always think back to the state of joy when I painted as a child. And that feeling of happiness is truly incomparable.

未命名 **纯粹的愉悦。**

陈 对，就是纯粹的愉悦，不掺杂任何东西。我在后来的探索里慢慢又找回来了以前纯粹的愉悦，很不想失去它们。

W&M Pure joy.

Chen Yes, pure joy, without any admixture. In my later explorations, I slowly regained the pure joy from my past, and I re ally don't want to lose it.

未命名 **曾经短暂的失去过，是吧?**

陈 是的，短暂的失去过。

W&M You lost it briefly, didn't you?

Chen Yes, briefly.

Art is a

艺术是一种效果

n effect

未命名 **你现在已经工作了是吧。**

张浩迪 对，现在大部分时间都在教学生画画，保证有一个基本的收入，剩下的时间做一点创作。

W&M So, you're working now, right?

Zhang Yes, most of my time is spent teaching students how to paint, ensuring a basic income, and using the remaining time for some creative work.

未命名 **有被学生的问题刁难过吗？**

张 现在主要教的是一些初中生，所以还好。慢慢找到了和他们相处的一种平衡。

W&M Have you ever encountered challenges from your students?

Zhang Currently, I mainly teach middle school students, so it's not too bad. I've gradually found a balance in dealing with them.

未命名 **你未来是想要租一个工作室还是有别的打算？**

张 我是在燕郊租了一个带房子的小院儿，成本不高，但是比较破，放了很多东西在那边。最近一直没有利用起来，以后可能会稍微修整一下作为我的一个小工作室。

W&M Do you plan to rent a studio in the future, or do you have other plans?

Zhang I've rented a small courtyard with a house in Yanjiao. The cost is not high, but it's a bit run-down, and I've stored a lot of things there. I haven't used it much lately, but I might fix it up a bit in the future and turn it into a small studio.

未命名 **你是想改造一下？**

张 是的，现在太破了，完全当仓库了。

W&M Are you thinking of renovating it?

Zhang Yes, it's too run-down now, basically functioning as a warehouse.

工作室一角
A corner of the studio

未命名 **到时候我们去帮你和水泥搬砖。**

张 没问题。（笑）

W&M When the time comes, we'll help you with the bricks and cement.

Zhang No problem, Haha!

未命名 **毕业之后你没有选择继续留在校园，去做一些批评或者史学的研究。**

张 对，我周围大多数人都是这样一个选择，我的话，还是想要在社会上待一待。在美院的环境里面，做任何创作可能都特别合理。做艺术，都是围绕着课程在走。那到了社会环境里，到我自己的生活里，艺术到底是一个什么样的存在？脱离学院的氛围和课程的推进，我有多少创作的热情，我的创作会走向什么方向？我觉得我需要先去试一试。

W&M After graduation, you didn't choose to stay on campus and engage in some critical or historical research, right?

Zhang That's right. Most people around me made that choice. As for me, I wanted to spend some time in society. Within the art academy, any form of creation seemed to make sense. And art creation revolved around the curriculums. But in the societal environment, in my own life, what exactly is the nature of art? Departing from the atmosphere of the institution and the progression of courses, how much passion for creation do I have, and in what direction my creations should go? I felt the need to go out and try.

未命名 **那现在转变开始了吗？**

张 现在就是没有那种被课程跟着的感觉了，有想法就去做。想停下来去做点其他的事情，我就停下来。转变倒是也没什么转变，就是在找自己的生活。

W&M So, is the transition happening now?

Zhang Totally. Now, there's no longer the feeling of following a syllabus. If I have an idea, I go ahead and do it. If I feel like stopping to do something else, I stop. The transition hasn't been significant; it's just about finding my own life.

未命名　你是从高中开始的创作吗？

张　高中就是国内普通的艺术高中，学的跟我现在教学生的内容差不多，素描之类的。

W&M　Did your creative journey start in high school?

Zhang　High school was just an ordinary art high school in China, studying something similar to what I teach my students now, like sketching.

未命名　学院式的教育对你影响最大的部分在哪儿呢？

张　还是做创作的过程吧！在课上做方案汇报，整理自己的想法，这个过程对我影响比较大，甚至可以说在不断塑造我的思维，包括怎么去认识这个世界，怎么去不断地挖掘自我意识，怎么去对周遭的事物作判断。现在总是在用一个创作者的视角去观察我自己和这个世界，在这个视角下，生活就是美术馆。

W&M　In what aspect did institutional education have the most significant impact on you?

Zhang　It's still the process of creating! Doing project presentations in class, organizing my thoughts—this process has had a significant impact on me. It has continuously shaped my thinking, including how to understand the world, how to constantly explore self-awareness, and how to judge the things around me. Now, I'm always observing myself and the world from the perspective of a creator, in which life is like an art gallery.

张浩迪的书桌

Zhang Haodi's desk

未命名　毕业之后，关于艺术，你身边的朋友也应该都有了新的选择。

张　有一些人，喜欢的和想做的东西正好就是市场或者大众更能接受的，我觉得很幸运，这样就不用太担心生存的问题。而大多数人还是走一步看一步，毕业之后基本又都去深造了。

W&M　After graduation, regarding art, your friends around you must have made new choices as well.

Zhang　For some people, what they like and want to do aligns perfectly with what the market or the public can readily accept. I feel that they're fortunate in that regard, as they don't have to worry too much about survival. However, most people take things one step at a time, and after graduation, they mostly go on to further studies.

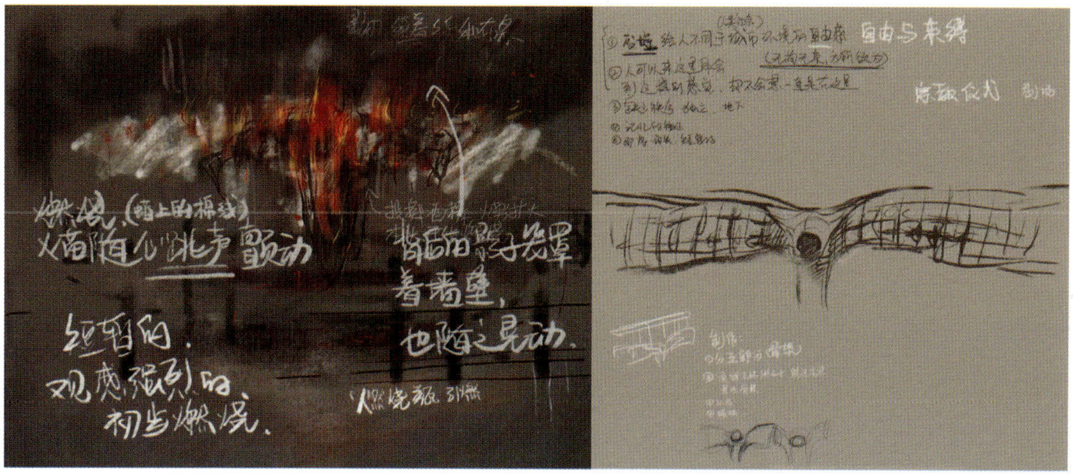

草稿 I

Sketch I

未命名　在学校里创作的这五年里所谓的那些奖项，不管是来自于学校内的或者学校外的奖有没有光顾过你？

张　有是有，但是比较少。

W&M　During your five years of creating in school, did any awards, whether from within or outside the school, come your way?

Zhang　There were some, but relatively few.

未命名　你会介意这个事吗？

张　这倒无所谓，能拿奖的人，他的性格就是能拿奖的性格，我就是拿不了奖的性格。（笑）

W&M　Do you mind that?

Zhang　Nah, not really. Those award-winners? They've got that winning personality. Me? I've got the personality that just ain't winning awards. Haha.

未命名　能不能描述一下你们工作室的工作流程。

张　每个老师都有不同的教学方法，比如说有的老师会让你一口气围绕一个动词出十个方案，接着再不断地去筛选，推进。有的会从公共事件着手，在调研中出方案。也有时从一个空间开始着手，或者从自我分析着手，等等。不过不管从哪着手，大体上的流程都是调研、汇报讨论、出稿、再讨论。

W&M　Could you describe the workflow in your studio?

Zhang　Every teacher has their own teaching methods. For instance, some teachers might have you come up with ten proposals centered around a verb in one go, then continuously filter and progress. Others might start with public events and develop proposals through research. Sometimes, it begins with a specific space or self-analysis, and so on. Regardless of the starting point, the general process involves research, presentation and discussion, drafting, and further discussion.

未命名 **你在做毕业作品《心底的群鸦》的时候，调研过哪些艺术家？**

张 我比较喜欢的孙原和彭宇的作品，他们做了很多动态装置的作品，对我影响比较大。这些作品构思巧妙，不论是视觉还是观念，都有足够的冲击力。还有就是让·丁格利的一些作品，他的作品有特别强烈的手工感，粗糙中蕴含着一种力量。

W&M When you were working on your graduation project, *Crows in the Heart*, which artists did you research?

Zhang I really like the works of Sun Yuan and Peng Yu. They've done a lot of dynamic installations that have had a significant impact on me. These pieces are cleverly conceived and pack a punch both visually and conceptually. Also, some works by Jean Tinguely – his pieces have a distinct handmade feel, with rawness that contains a certain power.

草稿 II　Sketch II

未命名 **你会特别关注从美院的教育系统中成长起来的艺术家吗？**

张 没有特别关心吧。包括国外的艺术家，我只会关注和深入了解一些对我会有所启发的艺术家。

W&M Do you pay special attention to artists who have grown from the education system of art institutes?

Zhang Not particularly. Including foreign artists, I only focus on and delve deeper into artists who inspire me.

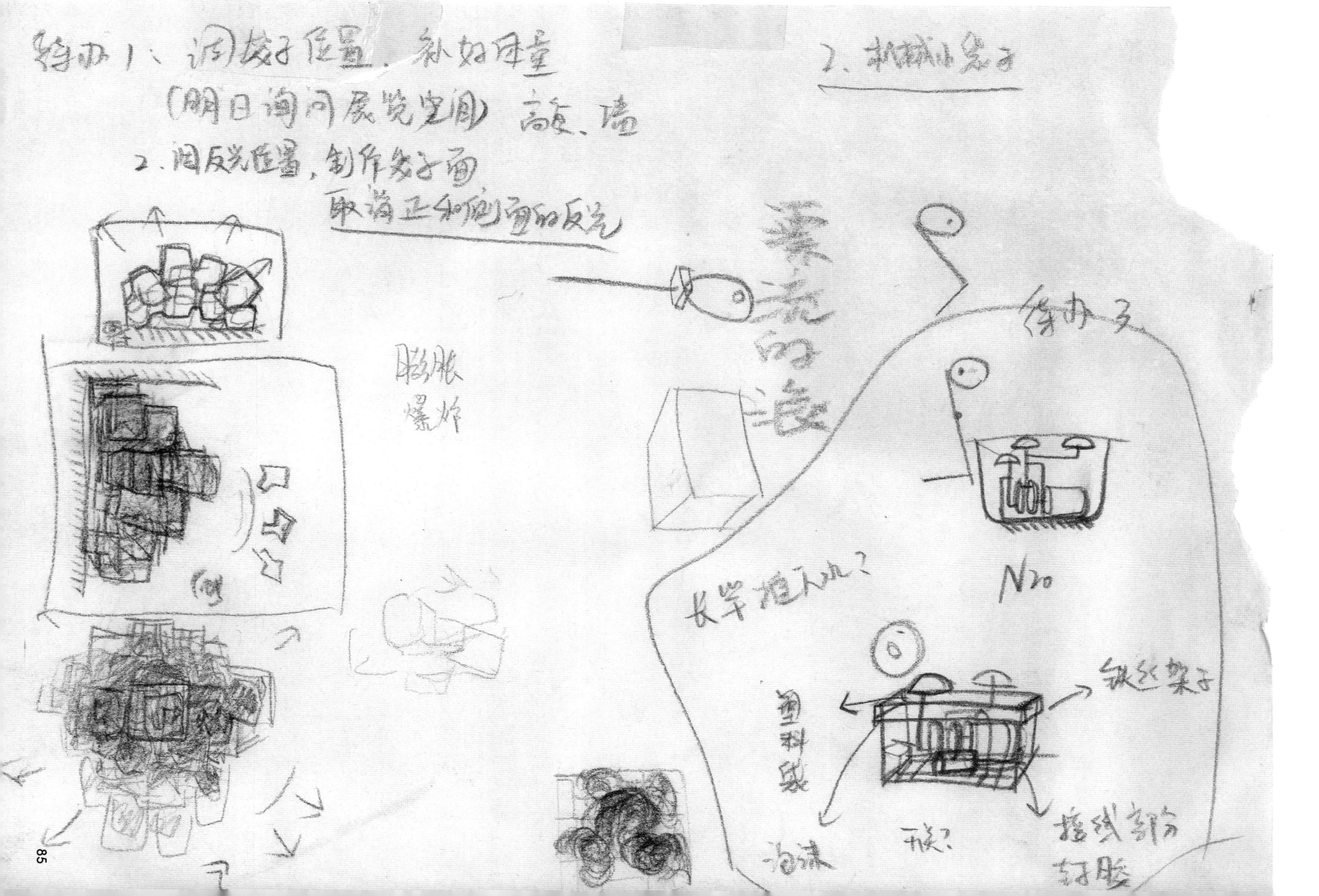
(明日询问展览空间) 高度、墙
取消正和侧面的反光
膨胀
爆炸
长竿插入水?
N20
铁丝架子
塑料感
接线部分
封胶
泡沫

未命名　**《心底的群鸦》这件作品的创意也是来自于课堂的讨论吗?**

张　准确地说，它是课程学习中延伸出来的。我们的学制是五年，我是在大四的时候开始对动态装置产生兴趣，相比静态的艺术，动态可以呈现出更大程度的视觉效果，减少作品和观众的距离，更容易刺激到人的感受。我沿着这个思路从身边寻找素材时，又关注到了“撕快递”的动作，觉得它是有一定隐喻性的动态。从完成作品的角度看，它会有很多的可能性，所以最终选择了它。在之后的创作里，通过单独的动态延伸出新的组装形式，以及开合的运动方式，然后围绕着视觉效果构建成了这样。

W&M　Is the creative idea for *Crows in the Heart* also from classroom discussions?

Zhang　To be precise, it's an extension of our course studies. Our program is five years long, and it was during my fourth year that I started getting interested in dynamic installations. Compared to static art, dynamic pieces can deliver a greater visual impact, reduce the distance between the artwork and the audience, and stimulate feelings more easily. As I explored this idea, I noticed the action of "tearing parcels" and found it to be a metaphorically dynamic action. Looking at the possibilities from the perspective of completing the work, I ultimately chose it. In subsequent creations, I extended new assembly forms through individual dynamics and opening-closing movements, and then built other parts based on their visual effects.

草稿 IV　　Sketch IV

未命名　**你当时在做这个作品时有没有为这个动作做过一些象征性的引申?**

张　有的，我觉得它毕竟不是一个纯抽象的东西。我使用了一个现成品，这个现成品与我的联系在哪里，我需要为它带来什么样的情绪？我第一个联想到的是消费，但并不想喊出各种关于消费主义与反消费的口号，而是把它当作我生成作品视觉的一个方向。所以几乎是完全考虑着形式来进行的，通过形式冲击到观众，剩下的部分再留给观众去想象。艺术品在观众身上引起的效果和艺术家想要表达的观念，这两者我是分开来看的。

W&M　Did you consider any symbolic extensions for this tearing-parcels action when creating this piece?

Zhang　Yes, I felt this action wasn't purely abstract. I utilized this readymade, and I need to consider where it connected with me and what emotions it should bring. My first association was with consumption, but I didn't want to shout out various slogans about consumerism or anticonsumerism. Instead, I treated it as a direction for visually shaping my artwork. So, I almost entirely considered the form to create an impact on the audience, leaving the rest for them to imagine. I separate the effects the artwork has on the audience from the concepts the artist wants to convey.

《心底的群鸦》
Crows in the Heart

《心底的群鸦》局部 I
Detail of *Crows in the Heart* I

《心底的群鸦》局部 II

Detail of *Crows in the Heart* II

未命名 **从创作的角度来看，现在的你会对这件作品有不满意的地方吗？**

张 造型上还需要一些调整，但现在还在大同那边展出，所以只能等到展览结束了，不过所呈现的效果还是满意的。

W&M From a creative perspective, are there aspects of this work that you are dissatisfied with now?

Zhang There are still some adjustments needed in terms of the design, but it's currently exhibited at Datong, requiring me to wait until the exhibition is over. However, I'm satisfied with the presented effect now.

未命名 **你会把自己放到一个竞争的环境里边吗，在班级里或者整个美院里给自己排个名？**

张 有，难免会有，我觉得我做得挺好的。好不谦虚（笑）。但我觉得《心底的群鸦》符合我对艺术的一种追求吧。我想在展览上看到这样一件作品，然后我把它做出来了。

对我而言，艺术就是恰好正在喜欢做的事情。它对我的价值追求和思维方式是有影响的，塑造了我现在的生活状态。

W&M Would you place yourself in a competitive environment, ranking yourself within the class or the academy?

Zhang Sure, it's inevitable. I think I did pretty well. Not to brag, ha-ha. But I feel *Crows in the Heart* aligns with my pursuit of art. I wanted to see such a piece at an exhibition, and I made it happen.

For me, art is precisely doing something I love. It influences my values and way of thinking, shaping my state of life.

《心底的群鸦》局部 III
Detail of *Crows in the Heart* III

未命名 **所以你未来是很坚定要成为艺术家吗？对这个身份你自己有没有什么特别的看法。**

张 我觉得未必会是一个职业艺术家，靠卖我的作品和签约艺术机构来为生，艺术更多的是作为平时生活的一种追求。我会通过观看和创作艺术来挖掘自己，然后用这个视角去观察和认识世界。

W&M So, are you firmly committed to becoming an artist in the future? Do you have any particular views on this identity?

Zhang I don't necessarily see myself as a professional artist, making a living by selling my works or signing with art institutions. Art is more of a pursuit in my everyday life. I explore myself through observing and creating art, using that perspective to observe and understand the world.

未命名 **毕业展览上，你的作品周围有特别多的观众，你有没有预想到这么多人对你的作品感兴趣。**

张 做这件作品之前有预想到会有很多人感兴趣。选择这样一个动态装置的形式，就是想让它和大众发生一些关系，不过也没有预想到有这么多人。

W&M During the graduation exhibition, there were a lot of people around your work. Did you anticipate so much interest in your work?

Zhang Before creating this piece, I did anticipate that many people would be interested. Choosing the form of a dynamic installation was meant to create a connection with the public, although I didn't expect such a large audience.

未命名 **这件作品在毕业展览期间，有没有给你带来一些合作？**

张 有很多人联系过我，除过受邀参加过两个展览，并没有实际产出什么内容。

W&M Did this work during the graduation exhibition lead to any collaborations for you?

Zhang Many people have contacted me. Although aside from being invited to participate in two exhibitions, there hasn't been any actual collaboration or output.

未命名 **大多数人很难在毕业之后立刻就成为一个艺术家，你对所处的艺术环境有什么看法？**

张 对于我做的非传统的创作，这个环境好像没那么友好，包括学校里面也是。有话语权的人还是倾向于认可他熟悉领域里的东西，我的想法与作品可能只能和年轻的朋友去交流，而年轻人可能又没有话语权。但我其实也没有想过通过作品获得什么样的成就，获得多少收入。现在参加展览，会有种做公益的感觉。就是在花很多的时间，花自己的钱，把自己觉得好的东西分享出去。这个过程中会结交到很多聊得来的朋友，也会得到许多交流与反馈，不过还是很难带来什么物质上的收入。

W&M For most people, it's challenging to immediately become an artist after graduation. What are your thoughts on the artistic environment you find yourself in?

Zhang For the non-traditional creations I pursue, the environment doesn't seem that friendly, including within the school. Those with influence tend to acknowledge things within their familiar domains. My ideas and works might only resonate with younger people, but they might not have much influence. However, I haven't really thought about achieving anything or earning income through my works. Participating in exhibitions feels more like doing charity. I spend a lot of time and my own money to share things I find valuable. In this process, I made many like-minded friends and received a lot of exchange and feedback. However, it's still challenging to bring in any material income.

未命名 **这个现象似乎很普遍。青年艺术家的作品变成了艺术展览空间里锦上添花的东西，艺术展览机构变成了一个艺术场的主角，艺术家变成了像买卖市集上的小摊贩，有时候甚至要自掏腰包。**

张 是这样的。

W&M This phenomenon seems to be quite common. The works of young artists have become the icing on the cake in the space of an art exhibition. The art institutions take on the roles of the main character in that scene, and artists have become like vendors in a marketplace, who sometimes even pay out of their own pockets.

Zhang Exactly.

未命名 **下一个作品你想要分享什么？**

张 已经着手在创作了，用了汽车轮胎作材料，想做出从既定位置逃逸而出的感觉，逃逸的轮胎。还是以达成效果为主，给观众一个强烈的效果，激发观看的人的情绪与联想。我会经常在一个小本儿上记录很多想法，并简单勾勾草图。不过找到材料后，更多还是会按照我自己当下的状态，在动手实验中去寻找想要的效果。

W&M On your next work, what would you like to share?

Zhang I'm already diving into a new project, using car tires as material. I want to capture the sensation of breaking free from a set position, escaping tires. Still, the main focus is on achieving an effect, giving the audience a strong impact, sparking emotions and associations. I often jot down lots of ideas and quick sketches in a small notebook. But once I find the materials, it's mostly about experimenting hands-on to achieve the desired effect based on my current state.

新作草图 I
The Sketch of new work I

未命名 **你刚刚多次提到了一个词，就是艺术的“效果”，这个好像是传统绘画或者说传统艺术里不太追求的东西。对你而言，它来自于哪里？**

张 关于效果，我认为它就是会刺激人感性上的东西，通过对感性的牵制让人进入对自我或者生活的思考，当然，后半部分有没有，可能也不要紧。当代艺术擅长营造效果。它有新鲜的、当下的艺术语言来适配当下的人的观看习惯，从而更顺利地击打出人的感受。同时，创作时的实验艺术精神也鼓励着观众去做出自我的感受和判断，等大众认识到这一点以后，大家从当代艺术中得到的感受该比传统作品更多。我对效果的追求，其实就是对作品和更多人发生关系的追求。我不想做那种封闭的作品，或者很自我，自娱自乐式的作品。我觉得好的作品该触及到人的共性，不管是视觉的共性还是情感的共性，从而使哪怕没怎么接触过艺术作品的大众也能从中得到感受。营造效果是个好办法，效果不分人，对谁都有效。

W&M You've mentioned a lot about the term “effect”, something not typically pursued in traditional painting or art. For you, where does it come from?

Zhang Regarding the effect, I think it's about stimulating something emotional in people. Through this emotional engagement, it prompts self-reflection or contemplation about life. Of course, whether that second part happens or not, it's not a big deal. Contemporary art excels at creating effects. It uses fresh, current artistic language to match contemporary people's viewing habits, hitting their feelings more smoothly. At the same time, the experimental spirit in artistic creation encourages the audience to make their own feelings and judgments. Once the public realizes this, they might get more from contemporary art than from traditional works. My pursuit of effect is essentially a pursuit of the artwork's connection with more people. I don't want to create closed-off or selfindulgent pieces. I believe good artwork should touch on something universal, be it visual or emotional, allowing even those who haven't had much exposure to art to feel something. Creating an effect is a good way — it doesn't discriminate; it works for everyone.

未命名 **某种意义上这是你的一种艺术观吧，用你做出来的艺术，跟所谓的艺术圈外的人发生一种互动和交流，他们的看法也许对你来说是更重要的。**

张 对，是这样。

W&M In a sense, this is your artistic philosophy. With your art, you're fostering interaction and communication with people outside the so-called art circle, and their perspectives might be more crucial for you.

Zhang Exactly.

未命名 **你对作品里的观念和自我主张保持一种冷静的克制，而不沉溺其中，这非常难得。**

张 最早应该是大二的时候，有一些涉及到关于自我表达的课程，我就一直在研究自己到底是什么样的人，在这之前也不会想这么多，大家怎么样，我就怎么样。从那之后可能就回不去了，不停地去考虑一些更自我的东西。

W&M You maintain a cool restraint when it comes to the concepts and self-assertion in your work, not getting lost in it. That's pretty rare.

Zhang It probably started around my sophomore year when I took courses related to self-expression. I've been trying to figure out who I really am since then. Before that, I didn't think much about it – just went with the flow. After that, maybe there's no turning back. I keep pondering more about something more personal.

未命名 **你的作品从自我的观察出发，但是最后的呈现是想跟大众多做一点沟通。不知道你对这个事有没有自觉？**

张 就是想要这样一个效果。我觉得把我的表达能传达给大众，也是我自我的一部分。有些人会只做他自己的东西，把自己的经历传达出来，不在乎他人的接受，别人看不看得懂都可能不重要。我不是这样的人。

W&M Your work stems from self-observation, but the ultimate presentation aims to communicate more with the public. Are you aware of that?

Zhang Exactly, I want that kind of effect. I feel that conveying my expression to the public is also a part of myself. Some people only create things for themselves, sharing their experiences without caring whether others understand or not. I'm not that kind of person.

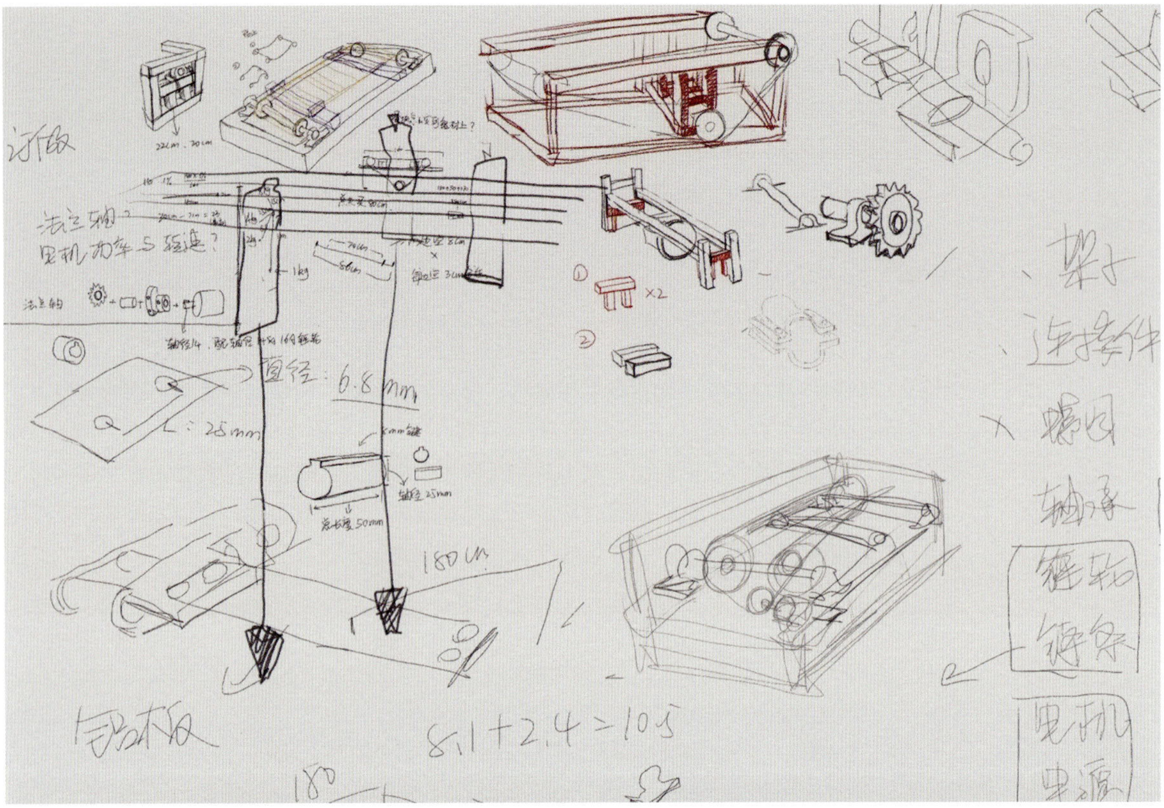

新作草图 II

The Sketch of new work II

未完成新作

Unfinished new work

未命名 **是的，其他一些艺术家似乎是在描述自己的个人经历，而你提炼出来了一个共性，你在描述大众共有的一个行动或姿态。《心底的群鸦》是对日常生活的一个转化，希望你能继续创作出有趣的作品。**

张 谢谢。

W&M Indeed, some artists seem to be describing their personal experiences, while you've distilled a commonality. You're portraying an action or posture that the public collectively shares. *Crows in the Heart* is a transformation of everyday life. Hope you keep creating interesting pieces.

Zhang Thank you.

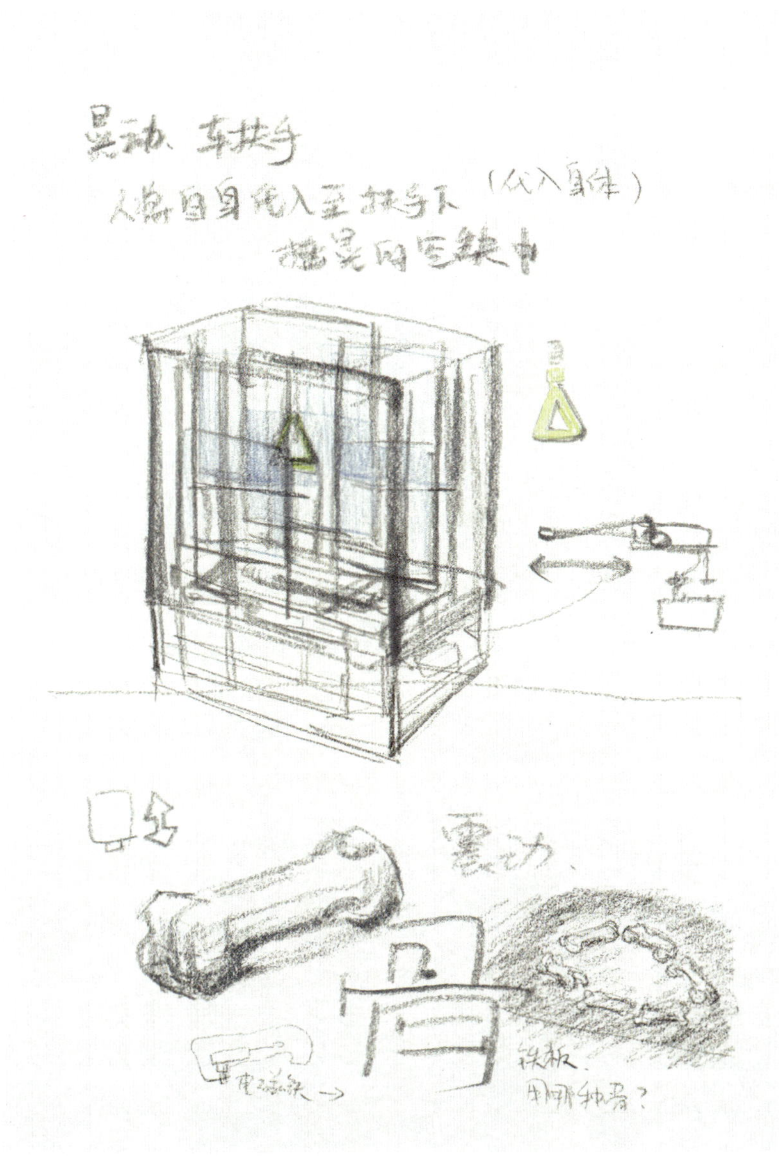

新作草图 III
The Sketch of new work III

未命名 **在艺术之外，你的生活大概是是什么样的呢？**

张 我是喜欢自己玩的那种人，朋友不那么多。我喜欢大自然，喜欢养小动物，现在生活比较稳定，就养了一只小狗。大学的时候养了一些蜥蜴、守宫，各种爬宠，偶尔还去钓鱼、爬山。都是老年人爱好。（笑）

W&M What is your life like outside of the art world?

Zhang I'm the kind of person who likes to play by myself, and I don't have that many friends. I love nature and raising small animals, and now that my life is more stable, I have a puppy. Back in college, I had some lizards, geckos, all kinds of reptile creatures, and occasionally went fishing and hiking. Pretty much the hobbies of an old man, ha-ha.

未命名 **最近还对什么感兴趣呢？**

张 因为现在需要上班挣钱，接触的世俗化的东西会多一点了，所以最近对冥想感兴趣多一些，看一些视频，每天会静坐一会儿。最近在读《巫士唐望的教诲》，对那种偏原始的玄学产生了一些兴趣。那些没有被现代文明社会所侵染太多的事物，能让我从当下暂时脱离。

W&M Is anything new catching your interest lately?

Zhang Since I need to work and make some money now, I've been exposed to more everyday stuff. So lately, I've developed an interest in meditation, watching some videos, and taking a few minutes each day to sit quietly. I've also been reading *The Teachings of Don Juan* recently, developing some interest in that kind of primal witchcraft. The things untouched by modern civilized society gave me a temporary escape from the present.

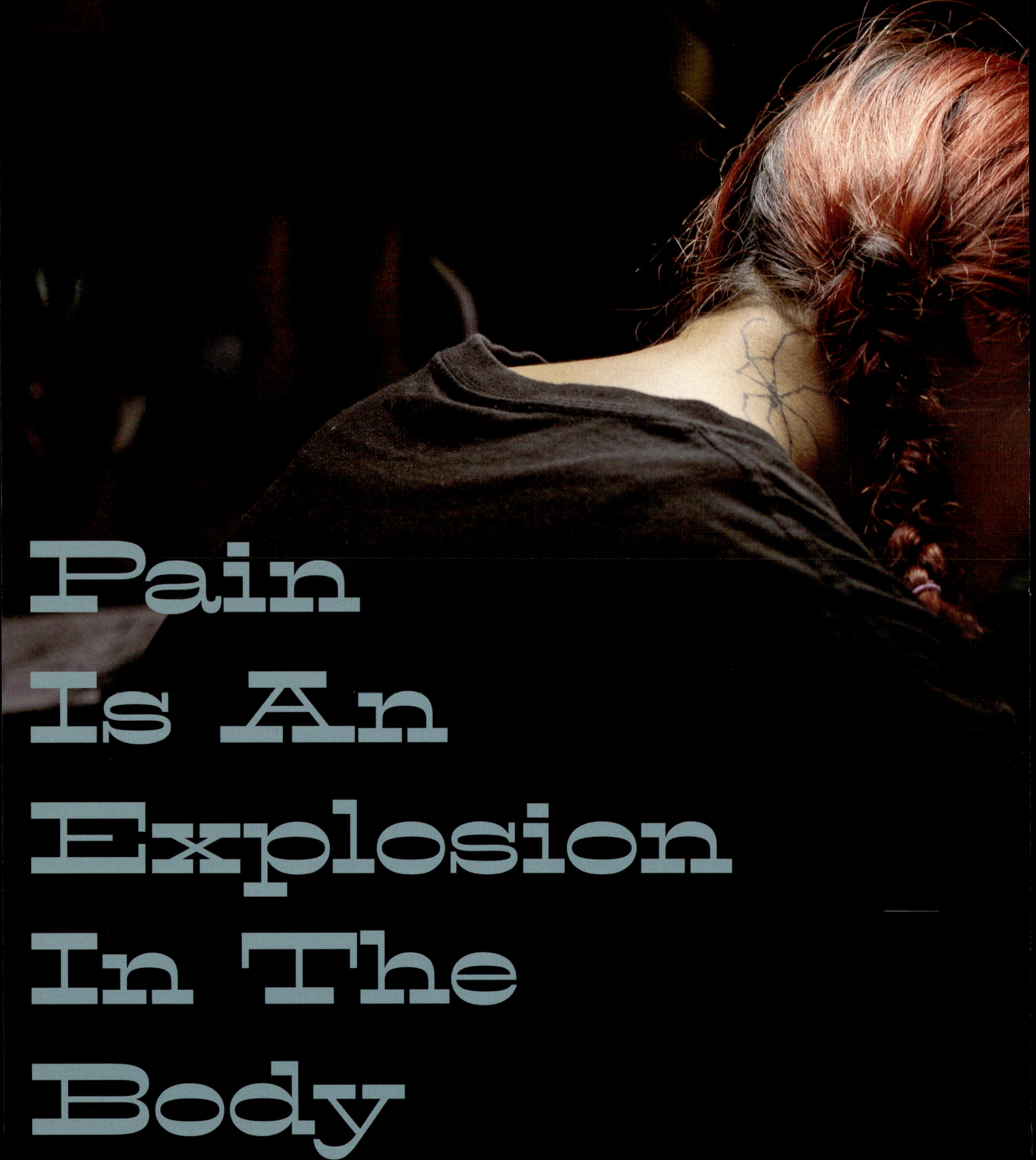

Pain Is An Explosion In The Body

疼痛是身体里的爆炸

贾童童：我所在的工作室主要研究东方雕塑，而我自己的创作更偏当代艺术。他们之间的差异其实并不大，都可以追溯到人类原始时代的行为，为此我专门写了一篇硕士论文，《肌肤之幕：从原始刺青到当代艺术》，就是把肌肤当成一个画布。我的很多创作灵感是从刺青这个行为中得到的，刺青对我而言是一种行为艺术。早在原始时期，人们就已经在皮肤上尝试创作。但我的创作更想关注刺青背后隐含的意义，以及被刺青者对于刺青的疼痛感受与状态。

Jia Tongtong: The studio I'm part of primarily focuses on Eastern sculpture, while my personal creations lean more towards contemporary art. The difference between them isn't significant and both can be traced back to primal human behaviors. For this, I wrote a master's thesis titled "Skin as a Canvas: From Primitive Tattoos to Contemporary Art", where I treat the skin as a canvas. Many of my creative inspirations stem from the practice of tattooing, which, for me, is a form of performance art. Back in primitive times, people were already experimenting with creating on their skin. However, my work aims to delve into the hidden meanings behind tattoos and the sensations and states experienced by those being tattooed.

未命名　您是如何把这种观念转化为创作的？

贾　《如果疼痛是种破碎的声音》其实源于我自己的生命体验，它看起来是一种破碎又聚合的状态。装置中间是一个人体，那是我自己的身体。我先用 3D 扫描打印，然后再用纸浆翻模，最后把它拼接成人形。人体的各个部分支离破碎，向周围扩散，在细线的拖拽下，又有一种上升的感觉，细线上挂满了文身用的针。展出的时候，纸张可能受潮了，视觉观感就没那么饱满。

我有自己的刺青工作室，接触了非常多喜欢文身的人，同时也记录下了他们对疼痛的感受与对文身的了解与看法。这些珍贵的意义被记录在日记本上，我把它叫作“疼痛日记”。

人对身体的感受其实来自于疼痛，但疼痛无法用语言描述。在自然的状态下，人通常不太关注身体的存在，只有在疼痛的时刻才会意识到身体的重要性，这背后跟心理学的机制有关，我的创作理念就建立在这个基础之上。

W&M　How did you translate this concept into your artwork?

Jia　*If Pain is a Shattered Sound* actually originated from my own life experiences, portraying a fragmented yet cohesive living state. In the center of the installation is a human body, my own body. I first used 3D scanning and printing, then molded it with papier-mâché, and finally assembled it into a humanoid form. The various parts of the body are fragmented, dispersing outward, and under the drag of fine threads, there's a sense of ascent. The fine threads are decorated with tattoo needles. During the exhibition, the paper might have absorbed moisture, affecting the visual impact.

I have my own tattoo studio, interacting with many tattoo enthusiasts. At the meantime, I documented their perceptions of pain and their understanding and opinions about tattoos. These valuable meanings are recorded in a diary I call *Pain Diary*.

Human awareness of their bodies often arises from pain, which cannot be described in words. In a natural state, people typically don't pay much attention to the existence of their bodies; it's only during painful moments that they become aware of the significance of their bodies. This is related to a psychological mechanism, and my creative philosophy is built upon this foundation.

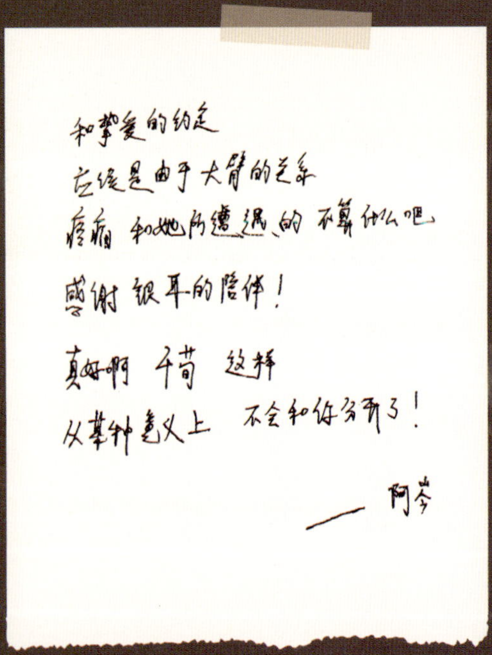

和挚爱的约定
应该是由于大臂的关系
疼痛和她所遭遇的不算什么吧
感谢银耳的陪伴！
真好啊 千荀 这样
从某种意义上 不会和你分开了！
——阿岑

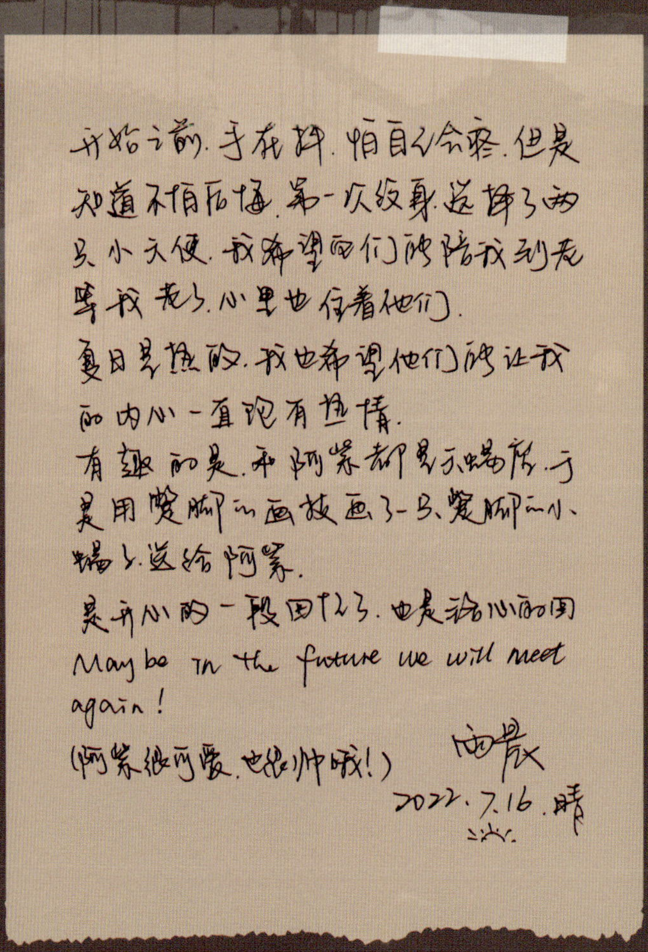

开始之前，手在抖，怕自己会疼，但是
知道不怕后悔。第一次纹身选择了两
只小天使，我希望它们能陪我到老
等我老了，心里也住着他们。
夏日是热的，我也希望他们能让我
的内心一直抱有热情。
有趣的是，我和阿紫都是小蝴蝶，于
是用蝴蝶的画技画了一只蝴蝶小
蝴蝶送给阿紫。
是开心的一段回忆了，也是铭心的回忆
Maybe in the future we will meet
again!
(阿紫很可爱，也很帅哦！)　西晨
2022.7.16.晴

未命名　**这种心理学的机制具体是什么呢？**

贾　在我看来，原始人类的潜意识依然留存于今天的行为艺术之中，当代的行为艺术家表面上对社会问题展开批判，揭示不公正的现象，但在其行为本身依然是生活在集体中的个人，通过艺术的途径释放内心压抑和恐惧。行为艺术从原始艺术和宗教艺术中获得某种观念与形式，它是社会群体意识的象征性表达和精神催眠。行为艺术家们通过视觉、触觉、嗅觉等其他的知觉形式，使得现代人的精神心理与原始人类的心理经验产生联结。

W&M　What specific psychological mechanisms are at play in this context?

Jia　In my view, the subconscious of primitive humanity still resonates in contemporary performance art. While contemporary artists outwardly critique societal issues, revealing injustices, while their actions are rooted in individual experiences within the collective. Through art, they release inner suppression and fear. Performance art draws certain concepts and forms from primitive and religious art, serving as symbolic expressions of societal consciousness and spiritual hypnosis. Artists utilize various perceptual forms such as vision, touch, and smell, establishing a connection between the psychological experiences of modern individuals and that of primitive humans.

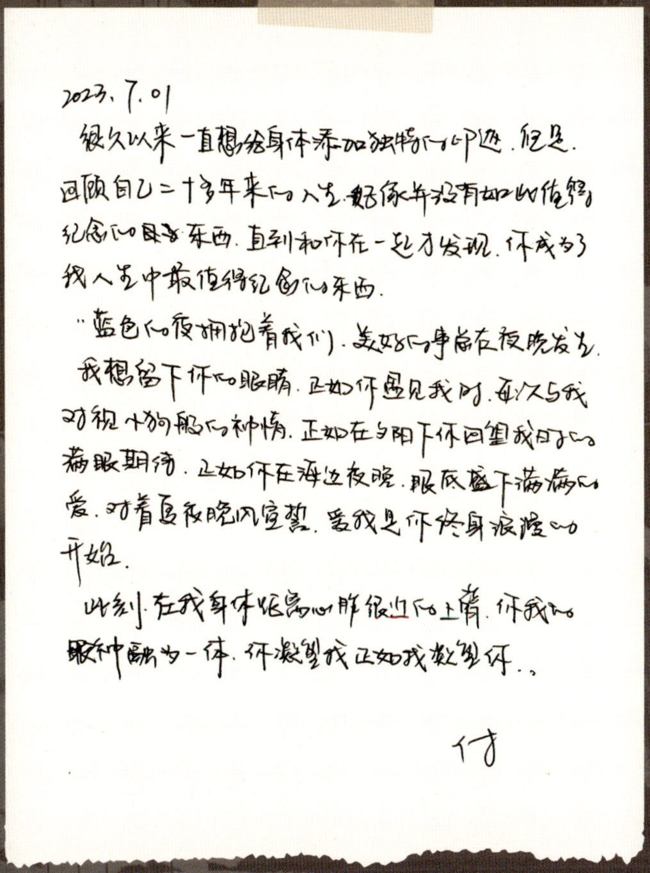

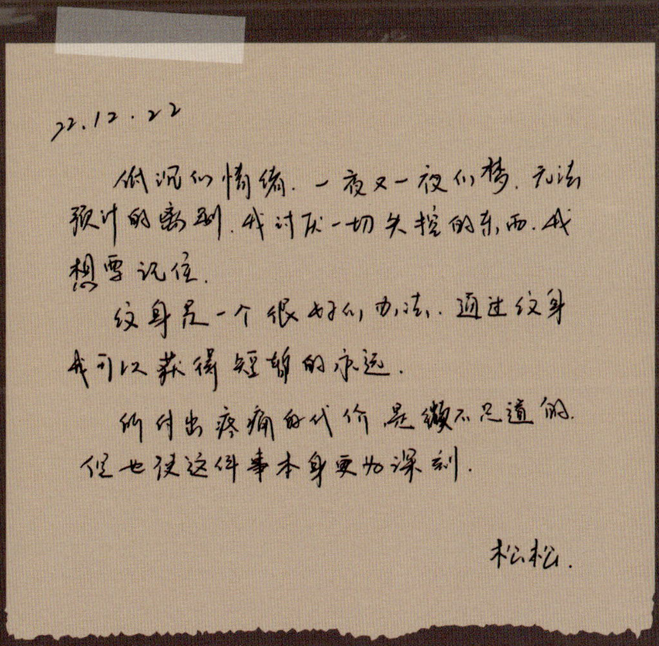

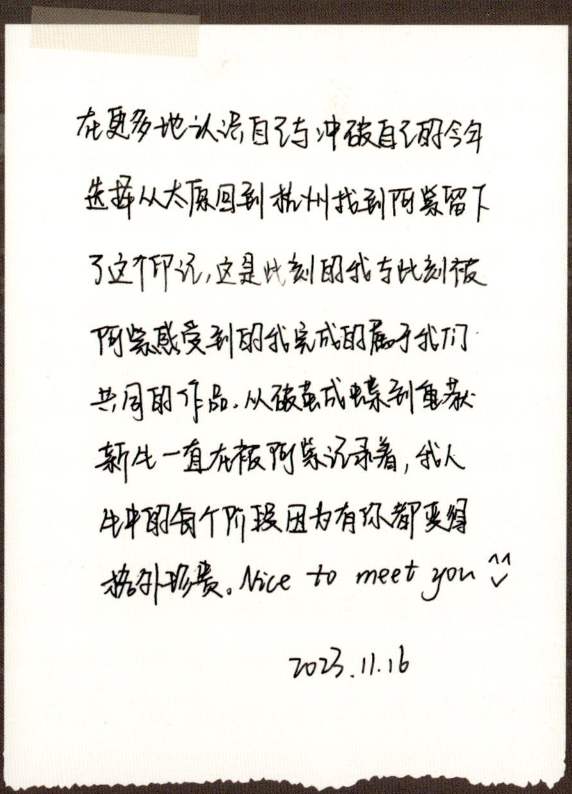

《疼痛日记》
Pain Diary

我经常觉得宇宙中的一切都是短暂的，无论是与人相遇，还是实在存在着的事实，这些不过是无数个短暂拼凑起来。而短暂加上短暂仍是短暂。每每想到此便觉得世界的无意义，万物终将凋落。但与阿岑相遇后，短暂的时间被神奇地拉长，并且有趣起来。阿岑是让我感受到我是切切实实活着的人。因此现在存于我身上的他是生命的一部分，鲜活的一部分，短暂中的永恒。他就像一株艾草一样，有着低饱和度的颜色，和淡淡的药草香味，是平凡中的特别，也是我迄今为止的人生中最真实的一部分，虚无中的具象。

2022.8.17

千简

"感觉自己在小学生谈恋爱"一直很想做纹身也从来没有下定决心，因为和小徐随口讲到就真的来做了。想起来，和她在一起仿佛做什么决定都变得果断而迅速，可能是爱给予的底气吧？

我一直很喜欢"宇宙"的概念，她广袤、浪漫、开阔、神秘、永恒，"纹身"本身也算是件永恒的事情，它永远停留在你的皮肤上，到死。我一直很向往，可以拥有一些象征又独特的意义。宇宙的神奇在于里面藏着数不清的悲欢离合和可爱事迹，有很多。

针尖刺入皮肤时，

我好像皮肉被剖开，任由色彩

流进血液，我的生命流了出来，

像花开在血管。

——小聪

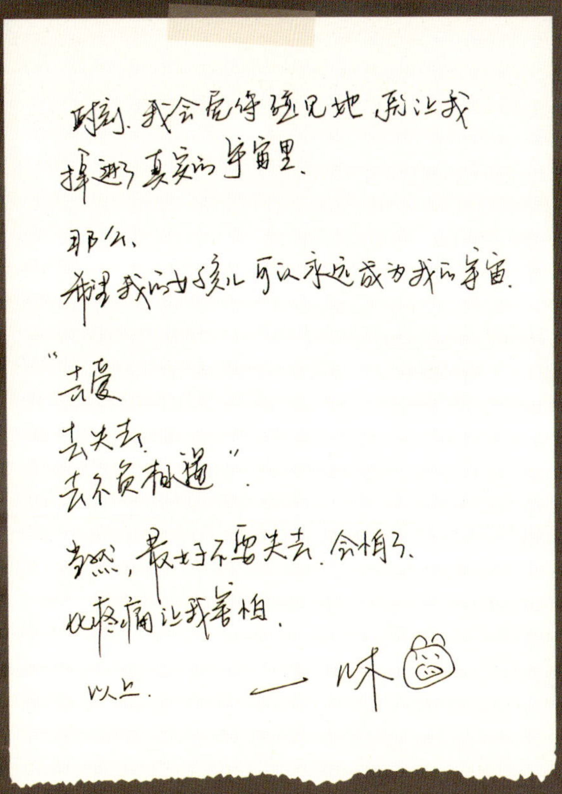

此刻，我会尽情地见她，然后让我
掉进了真实的宇宙里。

那么，
希望我的女孩儿可以永远成为我的宇宙。

“去爱
去失去
去不负相遇”。

当然，最好不要失去，会怕了。
比疼痛让我害怕。

以上。 —— 咻

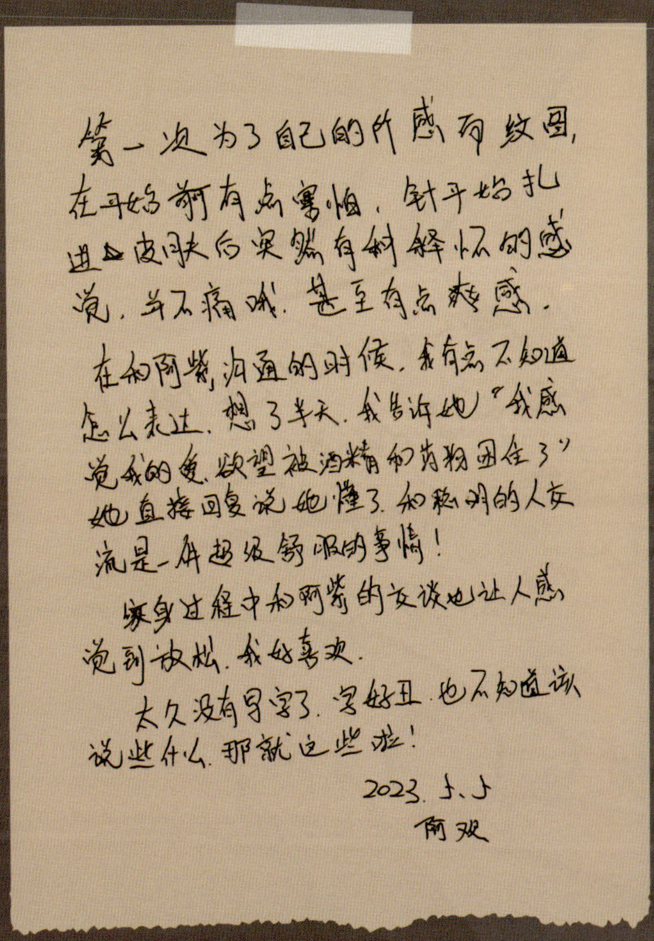

第一次为了自己的情感而纹图，
在开始前有点害怕，针开始扎
进皮肤后突然有种释怀的感
觉，并不痛哦，甚至有点爽感。

在和阿紫沟通的时候，我有点不知道
怎么表达，想了半天，我告诉她“我感
觉我的爱、欲望被酒精和药物困住了”
她直接回复说她懂了，和聪明的人交
流是一件超级舒服的事情！

纹身过程中和阿紫的交谈也让人感
觉到放松，我好喜欢。

太久没有写字了，字好丑，也不知道该
说些什么，那就这些啦！

2023.5.5
阿欢

未命名 **刺青是一种关于身体的技术，是物质化的，它会在文身者身上留下一些图腾符号。**

贾 我认为感受性是第一位的，图腾符号的意义倒是其次。符号是一个比较具象化的东西，它可能代表了生命当中的某一部分经历，也许是需要去纪念的人或事，也可能是自己的信仰。但疼痛更像是一种精神上的的体验，超越了符号和形式本身。我有时候也会引导被刺青者，他们的看法带给我很多灵感。

我曾经做过一个行为艺术，就是自己给自己文身。当时定下来用九个太阳的图案，我以空针，也就是不加任何颜色的方式，在自己的皮肤上穿刺。一直以来，我作为文身师都是在给别人施加疼痛，当这个过程由我自己来完成的时候，血液顺着针孔慢慢渗出，红色填充进了太阳的图案，那种感受无法用语言描述。

W&M Tattooing is a technical aspect related to the body, a materialization that leaves symbolic totems on the tattooed person.

Jia I believe sensitivity comes first, while the meaning of symbolic totems follows. Symbols are relatively concrete and may represent a part of life, perhaps commemorating a person or event, or expressing personal beliefs. However, pain is more like a spiritual experience that transcends symbols and forms. Sometimes, I guide those getting tattooed, and their perspectives provide me with a lot of inspiration.

I once performed a piece of performance art, tattooing myself. I decided on a pattern of nine suns, using an empty needle, meaning without adding any dye, piercing my skin. As a tattoo artist who usually inflicts pain on others, when I did it to myself, blood slowly seeped out along the needle holes, filling the sun pattern with red. That sensation is indescribable in words.

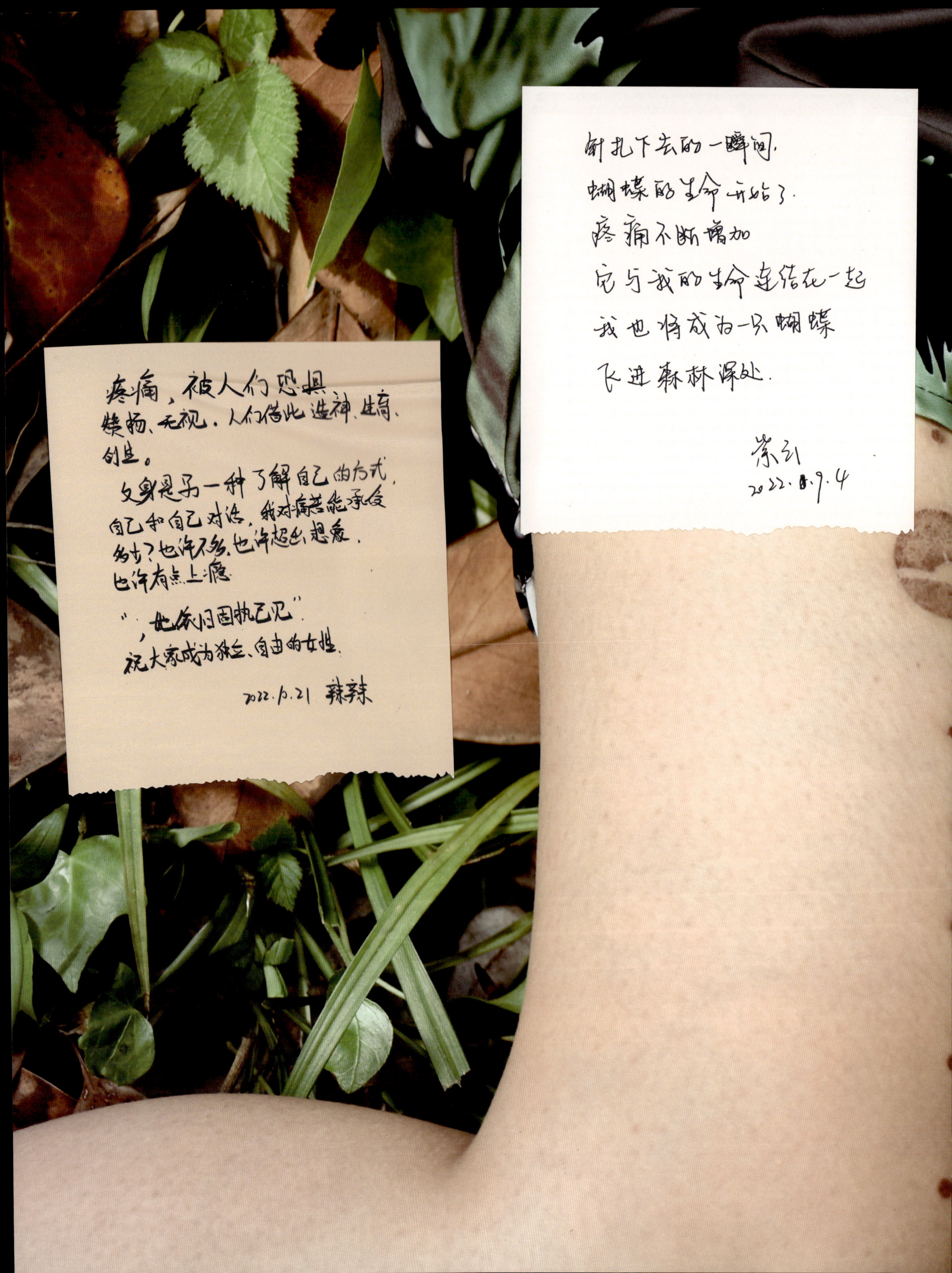
疼痛，被人们恐惧
嫉妒、无视，人们借此造神、生育、
创造。
文身是另一种了解自己的方式，
自己和自己对话，我对痛苦能承受
多少？也许不多，也许超出想象，
也许有点上瘾
"，她依旧固执己见"
祝大家成为独立、自由的女性
2022.6.21 辣辣
针扎下去的一瞬间，
蝴蝶的生命开始了，
疼痛不断增加
它与我的生命连结在一起
我也将成为一只蝴蝶
飞进森林深处。
崇引
2022.9.4

22.12.17
第一个纹身有特殊意义，之后第二、第三个，更多是一种压力的舒解。文完第二个，三四天没有好睡眠；第三个，走出工作室已经快要虚脱了。但那时候，我偏执地想从疼痛里找快乐。所以还好。
这是我的第四个纹身，我发现疼痛无法再带给我快乐了。所以我想，现在的我是不是更爱自己一点了？
小陈

纸模局部
Detail of Papier-mâché

未命名 **后来在毕业作品里为什么要用纸浆来作皮肤，这种材料的特殊性在哪？**

贾 纸浆很轻盈，可塑性也比较强，如果做成薄薄一层，就很像皮肤的质感。我之前也做了很多传统的实体雕塑，比如玻璃钢，石膏，金属，木头，还有其他的材料。我曾经用石膏来给自己的身体翻模，它能够非常细致地还原皮肤的纹理，但还是太坚硬了。我的导师一直在研究陶，艺术家可以利用这种材料烧制出不同的颜色，在视觉上有一种温度感，很亲近人。但它们之间有一种共性，那就是坚硬，很难表达我对疼痛的理解。描述疼痛可以用抽象的语言，但真切的疼痛只能自己感受。

这个过程的确蛮痛苦的，我一直在选材料，这些材料要符合主题，又要契合刺青的观念。那个时候的我，就像一个孤单的巫师，一个人建立起了一套巫术体系，完全由我自己主导。

W&M Why did you choose to use papier-mâché for the skin in your graduation project, and what is the uniqueness of this material?

Jia Papier-mâché is lightweight and has strong malleability. If crafted into a thin layer, it closely resembles the texture of skin. I've worked with various traditional sculpting materials like fiberglass, plaster, metal, wood, and others. I previously used plaster to make a mold of my body, capturing intricate details of the skin texture, but it was too rigid. My supervisor's research focus was on ceramics, a material that artists can use to fire different colors, offering a visual warmth and intimacy. However, they share a common characteristic of being hard, making it challenging to express my understanding of pain. Describing pain can use abstract language, but the true experience of pain can only be felt.

The process was indeed quite painful, and I was constantly selecting materials that aligned with the theme while capturing the essence of tattooing. At that time, I felt like a solitary wizard, establishing a system of magic entirely directed by myself.

未命名　很多参展的观众都很喜欢这件作品。

贾　我在社交媒体上也发布过这件作品，大家的感受都很不一样，他们会联想到各种不同的东西。这件作品还有一个基座，在漂浮的身体下方，床上还镶嵌了一面镜子。很多人以为这是一个病床，也有人以为我在还原做梦的状态。我在创作的时候，其实都没有做过这样的预设，也并不想把它呈现为一种所谓“美”的状态。我的生活状态可能比较消极，我一直很崇尚“消极美学”。

W&M　Many visitors at the exhibition really appreciate your work.

Jia　I also shared this artwork on social media, and people had varied reactions, associating it with different things. The piece includes a base with a mirror embedded beneath the floating body. Some viewers thought it resembled a hospital bed, while others believed I was recreating a dreamscape. When creating it, I didn't have such preconceptions, nor did I intend to present it as a so-called "beautiful" state. My outlook on life tends to be somewhat pessimistic, and I've consistently embraced a "negative aesthetics".

未命名　什么是“消极美学”？

贾　宏观来说，人类历史的发展充满着悲剧，消极的事物所产生的影响非常强大。如果回到现实，很多艺术家的创作其实是在消极痛苦的状态下完成的。有一种“侘寂美学”，近几年颇受大家欢迎，它所呈现出来的就是特定环境中的消极美。“消极美学”是一种直观的生活方式，接受自然的生死循环，强调在不完美中发现美，与小乘佛教的思想也有关系。

W&M　What is "Negative Aesthetics"?

Jia　In a broader sense, human history is full of tragedies, and the impact of negative elements is profoundly influential. Bringing it back to reality, many artists create in a state of negation or painful emotions. There's a trend called "Wabi-sabi aesthetics", which has gained popularity in recent years, expressing negativity in specific environments. "Negative aesthetics" is an intuitive way of life, accepting the cyclical nature of life and death, emphasizing finding beauty in imperfection, and it's also related to the principles of Mahayana Buddhism.

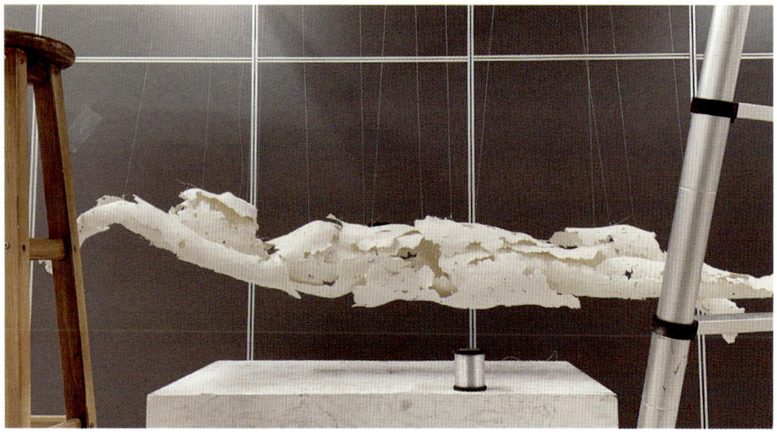

《如果疼痛是种破碎的声音》
If Pain is a Shattered Sound

未命名　**为什么起名叫《如果疼痛是种破碎的声音》？**

贾　文身的时候，疼痛会让人发出声音，这些声音，也是刺青的一部分。

W&M　Why did you choose the title *If Pain is a Shattered Sound*?

Jia　During tattooing, pain often elicits sounds, and these sounds become part of the tattoo.

未命名　有没有具体的艺术家或作品给你的创作带来灵感？

贾　当然有。华裔女艺术家刘北立做过一个名为《补缮工程》的行为作品。她将1500把剪刀悬挂在头顶，而艺术家却悠然自得地在剪刀下面缝着针线活，坚硬尖锐的剪刀与温和静谧的个体行为之间产生了强烈的冲突。每一个观众进入展厅的时候，都会将入口处的白布切下来带给艺术家，艺术家再将这些白布缝合，随着时间的推移，整个场所只剩下踩缝纫机与呼吸声，你会进入到沉思的状态，审视生命的意义。

行为艺术家之母玛丽娜·阿布拉莫维奇在《托马斯的嘴唇》(1975) 里，用剃须刀在肚子上割了一个五角星的图腾。还有乌雷的作品，他为了追寻自己的真实身份，在表演摄影的创作中加入了文身、切割、移植等方式。他先请文身师在自己的左臂上文上文字，然后找了一位医生将这个文身切下来，最后在艺术市场上出售。

还有很多艺术家给我留下很深的印象，不过对我的作品而言，我还是得回归到我的精神状况。

当时也有人跟我说，最后的效果有点像盐田千春的作品，虽然说有些材料上面可能有点相似，但其实我没有受她的影响。我为什么选择用黑线，是因为在刺青图案当中，黑色是表达最多的颜色。我对人体的处理又需要表达悬浮上升的状态，所以就采用了垂坠的线条。

W&M　Did any specific artists or works inspire your creations?

Jia　Certainly. Chinese-American artist Beili Liu created a performance piece called *The Mending Project*, where she suspended 1,500 pairs of scissors overhead while calmly sewing beneath them. The stark contrast between the sharp, rigid scissors and the gentle, serene act of sewing created a powerful conflict. Each visitor entering the exhibition would cut a piece of white cloth at the entrance and give it to the artist. Over time, the artist stitched these white pieces together. As the room filled with the sound of sewing machines and breathing, you'd enter a contemplative state, examining the meaning of life.

And Marina Abramović, the mother of performance art, in *Lips of Thomas (1975)*, cut a pentagram totem into her stomach with a razor blade. Ulay, another artist, explored his true identity through performance photography, incorporating tattoos, cutting, and transplants. He had a tattoo artist inscribe text on his left arm, then had a doctor cut it off and sold it in the art market.

Many artists left a deep impression on me, but for my works, I always return to my mental state.

Some suggested my final effect resembled Chiharu Shiota's work. Although there might be some material similarities, I wasn't influenced by her. I chose black lines, because in tattoo patterns, black expresses the most. Handling the human body required portraying a suspended and rising state, hence the use of descending lines.

未命名 **中国民间艺术里有很多对于线的处理，比如刺绣和针织，你有过这方面的联想吗？**

贾 有的，比如说用线把软材料跟质地更为坚硬的陶和石膏结合在一起，之前做了很多类似的尝试。

W&M In Chinese folk art, there's a lot of emphasis on line work, such as embroidery and knitting. Did you draw any inspiration from these?

Jia Yes, for instance, using lines to connect soft materials with harder textures like clay and plaster. I've experimented with similar approaches before.

未命名 **你的作品几乎都用到了新的数字技术，这是你自觉的探索吗？**

贾 我愿意去尝试一些新东西，跟这个时代的变化与大环境有关吧。

W&M Your works almost always involve new digital technologies. Is this a deliberate exploration on your part?

Jia I'm willing to try new things, which might be related to the changes in this era and the broader environment.

未命名 **同样做一件有关身体的雕塑，那你觉得 3D 扫描打印的方式，与传统雕塑的方式，哪一个更准确一些？**

贾 我认为还是泥塑做出来的会更有意思，这样做出来的作品是有生命力的。不过要看需要什么样的材料去表现个人的思考与情感吧，能够表达出内核就是好的。

W&M Creating a sculpture related to the body, do you think 3D scanning and printing or traditional sculpting is more accurate?

Jia I believe sculptures made from clay would be more interesting; they have vitality. However, it depends on the materials needed to express personal thoughts and emotions; what matters is conveying the core.

未命名 **疼痛似乎是你艺术创作的某种源起，你对疼痛的感知也比常人更丰富一些。**

贾 我感觉艺术创作是循序渐进的，也许一开始就有了某种感觉，但是没有办法把它变成现实，用合适的媒介材料把它表现出来。它开始于一次精神上的挣扎，自相矛盾的情感。

真正让我对疼痛有不一样的体验，跟我身上发生的一场意外有关。大二那年，我出了一场车祸。在那之后，我开始不断做梦，现在也是。恢复期间，我读了很多卡尔·荣格研究梦境和心理学的书，也画了很多与疼痛有关的水彩画。

疼痛对我而言，就是发生在我身体里的爆炸。我选择用具象的水彩画来描绘它，但呈现出的状态又是抽象的状态。

W&M Pain seems to be a source of inspiration for your artistic creations. Your perception of pain appears to be richer than that of the average person.

Jia I feel that artistic creation is gradual. Perhaps there's an initial sensation, but it's challenging to materialize it, to express it through the right medium and materials. It starts with a mental struggle and contradictory emotions.

My unique experience with pain is related to an accident that happened to me. In my sophomore year, I had a car accident. After that, I started having continuous dreams, which persist to this day. During the recovery period, I read a lot of Carl Jung's books on dream analysis and psychology and created many watercolor paintings related to pain.

Pain, for me, is like an explosion happening within my body. I chose to depict it through representational watercolors, but the result is abstract.

疼痛水彩 I

Watercolor of Pain I

未命名 **您应该尝试过很多种方式来治愈这次创伤吧？**

贾 我曾经去过道观，研究过自己的生辰八字。但我觉得还是跟人的心理有关。我很喜欢荣格的《红书》，他在这本书中描绘了非常多的梦境，甚至还预知到了战争的爆发。他一方面分析自己，另一方面也会医治别人的心理。我后来也尝试在文身中回应自己。刺青就是一种仪式，它的产生与祭祀和巫术有很大的联系，古代的人利用刺青来表达自己的情感，现在的人也是如此。在儒家文化里，刺青曾经被当成一种惩罚，或者被简化成恶人的象征。不同的历史时期，不同的区域，它的意义总是在变动。今天的亚文化中，文身又代表着一种生活方式。

W&M You must have tried various methods to heal from this trauma.

Jia I visited Taoist temples, and studied my own astrological chart. But I think they're more related to the human psyche. I really like Jung's *The Red Book*, where he describes numerous dreams, even predicting the outbreak of wars. He analyzes himself on one hand and heals others' psyches on the other. Later, I tried to respond to myself through tattoos. Tattooing is a kind of ritual, closely linked to ritual sacrifice and shamanism. People in the past used tattoos to express their emotions, and contemporary people do the same. In Confucian culture, tattoos were once considered a form of punishment or simplified as a symbol of evildoers. Across different historical periods and regions, its meaning always evolves. In today's subcultures, tattoos represent a way of life.

未命名 **您在做文身工作的时候，应该接触了很多情绪比较敏感的人吧？**

贾 非常多，对我与被刺青者而言，文身是一个治愈的过程。在这个过程中，二者缺一不可。在刺青的行为结束之后的某一个瞬间，他们真的可能会对自己有更多的了解，或者在情绪上找到了新的出口。我把这些情感都记录在《疼痛日记》里，这本日记也是我作品的一部分。

W&M When you were doing tattoo work, you must have encountered many emotionally sensitive individuals?

Jia A lot. For both myself and those receiving the tattoo, it's a healing process. Both parties are indispensable in this process. At a certain moment after the tattooing is done, they might truly gain more understanding of themselves or find new emotional outlets. I document these emotions in my *Pain Diary*, which is also part of my artwork.

未命名 **我相信他们也能从你的文身艺术上得到一些精神上的安慰。**

贾 对，所以我导师有时候就说，我就像当代巫师一样。（笑）

W&M I believe they can find some spiritual comfort from your tattoo art.

Jia Yes, that's why my mentor sometimes says I'm like a contemporary wizard. Haha.

疼痛水彩 II
Watercolor of Pain II

未命名 **文身时的图案是被文身者自己提供的，还是你自由发挥？**

贾 都有的，大多数人都是给我提供自己的想法，比如给出几个关键词，剩下的我来发挥就行。

W&M Are the tattoo designs provided by the person getting the tattoo, or do you have creative freedom?

Jia It varies. Most people provide their own ideas, giving a few keywords, and I take it from there.

未命名 **这个时候你会如何对待他们的身体？**

贾 他们会跟我讲述自己的情感故事，或者精神状态，跟我沟通。听完他们的故事，我会更了解他们一点，设计出理想的图案，最后再根据人体的部位来选择刺青。

W&M How do you approach their bodies during this process?

Jia They would share their emotional stories or their mental activities, communicate with me. After hearing their stories, I understand them a bit more and design an ideal pattern, choosing the tattoo based on the location of their body.

未命名 **当你的作品出现在公共展览之中，评价你作品的声音也越来越多元，你怎么看待这些评价？**

贾 完全不会在意。我的导师曾经提议我把基底的镜子打碎，如果镜子碎了，我获得的可能就是银奖，而不是铜奖。老师可能是出于整体的效果才提出这样的建议，但是我不想打碎。对我而言，镜子意味着另外一个空间，主体本身已经支离破碎了，如果镜子也是如此，这就脱离了我的艺术观念。

W&M As your works appear in public exhibitions, there are increasingly diverse opinions about your work. How do you view these evaluations?

Jia I don't care at all. My mentor once suggested that I should shatter the base's mirror. If the mirror is broken, I might get a silver award instead of a bronze one. My mentor probably proposed this for the overall effect, but I don't want to break it. For me, the mirror represents another space, and if it shatters too, it deviates from my artistic concept.

未命名 **老师的意思有种拉康心理学的意味，破碎的镜子加上破碎的主体，有种毁灭一切的悲痛。但这样的处理或许对你太极致了，并不是你想要的效果。**

贾 也许破碎的事物才会更有深刻性，不断地打破重塑再打破再重塑。在这个过程中会更加地认识这个世界以及自己。破碎的力量非常强大，如同喜剧的内核是悲剧一样，二者是合二为一的。

W&M The teacher's suggestion seems to have a Lacanian psychological implication, the shattered mirror combined with the fragmented subject, portraying a kind of sorrowful destruction. However, such an approach might be too extreme for you and not the effect you desire.

Jia Perhaps shattered things can be more profound, whilst continually breaking and reshaping. This process allows for a deeper understanding of the world and oneself. The power of fragmentation is immensely strong, much like how the core of comedy is tragedy; the two are intertwined.

未命名 **你的性格一直就是这样吗？**

贾 对，我是这样的，他甚至对我的评价是我很轴，有时候会钻牛角尖，就是不愿意做改变。

W&M Has your personality always been like this?

Jia Yes, that's how I am. His comment on me is that I'm very stubborn, sometimes nitpicking, just unwilling to change.

疼痛水彩 III
Watercolor of Pain III

未命名 **做完《如果疼痛是种破碎的声音》之后，你又做了新的作品。这件作品是在表达什么呢？**

贾 当时我的导师推荐我参加中国丝绸博物馆举办的“宋韵”展览，参展的作品全是雕塑。在我的艺术观里，人本身也是一个容器，人把自己的情感、情绪都藏在自己的身体里。玻璃瓶、陶罐，它们也可以承载很多东西，跟人有一种共通性。人有情感，物体也是有情感的。

W&M After completing *If Pain is a Shattered Sound*, you created new works. What does this piece express?

Jia At the time, my mentor recommended me to participate in the Rhyme of Song Dynasty exhibition held at the China Silk Museum, where all the exhibited works were sculptures. In my artistic perspective, a person is also a container; individuals hide their emotions and feelings within their bodies. Glass bottles, ceramic jars—they can also carry many things, sharing a commonality with humans. People have emotions, and objects have emotions too.

未命名 **这个作品花了多长时间？**

贾 很短时间就做出来了，但是思考构建整个作品花了大量的时间。过程可能才是最重要最有意义的。作品最后的呈现也并不是最后的结果，我一直觉得我做的是一件行为作品。（笑）

W&M How long did it take to create this piece?

Jia While the physical creation was quick, a significant amount of time was spent on contemplating and constructing the entire work. The process is probably the most important and meaningful part. The final presentation of the work is not the ultimate outcome; I have always felt that what I created was a performance art piece. Haha.

未命名 **你通过《如果疼痛是种破碎的声音》来剖析自己，讲述自己的故事，讲述自己的疼痛。**

贾 就把自己解剖开来，把自己撕裂解剖开来，看看到底有什么东西在里面。

W&M You dissected yourself through *If Pain is a Shattered Sound*, telling your story and expressing your pain.

Jia I dissected myself, tore myself apart to see what was inside.

未命名 **度过艰难时期最好的方法，似乎都是回到自己，以自己作为方法。**

贾 以自己为出发点是最直观最真实的，你不能用别人的东西来表达自己的观念，你只能从自己出发，你感受到的东西，你经历的东西，才成就了自己。

W&M The best way to get through difficult times seems to be returning to oneself, using oneself as a method.

Jia Starting from oneself is the most direct and authentic approach. You can't express your ideas with other people's things; you can only start from yourself, what you feel, what you experience—these are the things that eventually shape you.

失语者的荒诞

未命名 **在毕业作品的展览上，观众对你们的作品展示出很大的好奇心，很愿意参与到你们的交互式设计中。这是在选题阶段就想达到的效果吧？**

王亚楠 当时并没有预料到会有这么多人来体验。最开始确定这个主题的时候，学校要求我们每人提交一个方案上去。我的方案叫作《我与我周旋》，讲的是短视频的“爱欲机制”。我想问的问题是，为什么人会被短视频裹挟，这背后的技术原理是什么？艺翔的方案叫《深海》，他提出了一个社会模型叫“深海困境”，讲的是失语者所在的环境，有比较深的人文思考。在他的方案中，能看到我们毕业作品的创意雏形。

最后在老师的建议下，我们两个人决定共同做一件作品，探讨“短视频里的失语困境”。

徐艺翔 “深海困境”这样一个概念，其实就是我自己的一种生活体验。不管是在学校里，还是在社会上，总会存在着这样一种关系。我打个比方，我们现在要选出一个班长，候选人不一定具备当班长的潜质，但是因为有一部分人认可他，之后就会有其他人跟风投票，最后他成功当选。不认可他的人，连同跟风投票的人，这个时候都变成了“失语者”。这个过程他们自己也许也意识不到。

当我们的社会需要真实的意见反馈时，“失语者” 真正的声音慢慢被掩盖掉。可以发表意见的人却不去表达真实，所采取的行动也并不是其他人真正需要的。最后导致沟通的困境越来越深，就像深海一样，一层一层，看不见底。“失语者”的看法不断被误解，慢慢就消失在了社会之中，没有人再去关注。

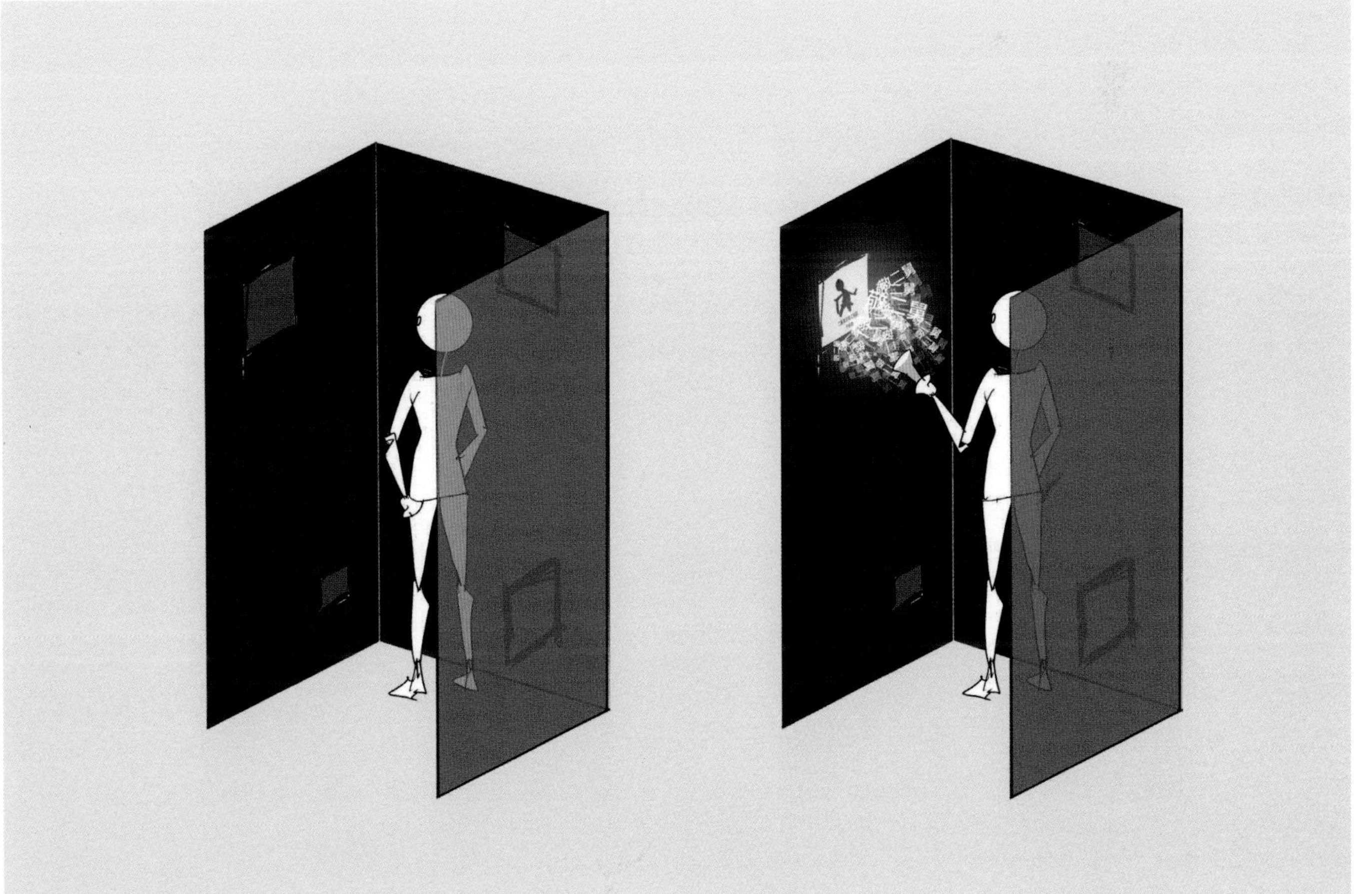

设计草图 I　Sketch I

THE ABSURDITY OF THE VOICELESS

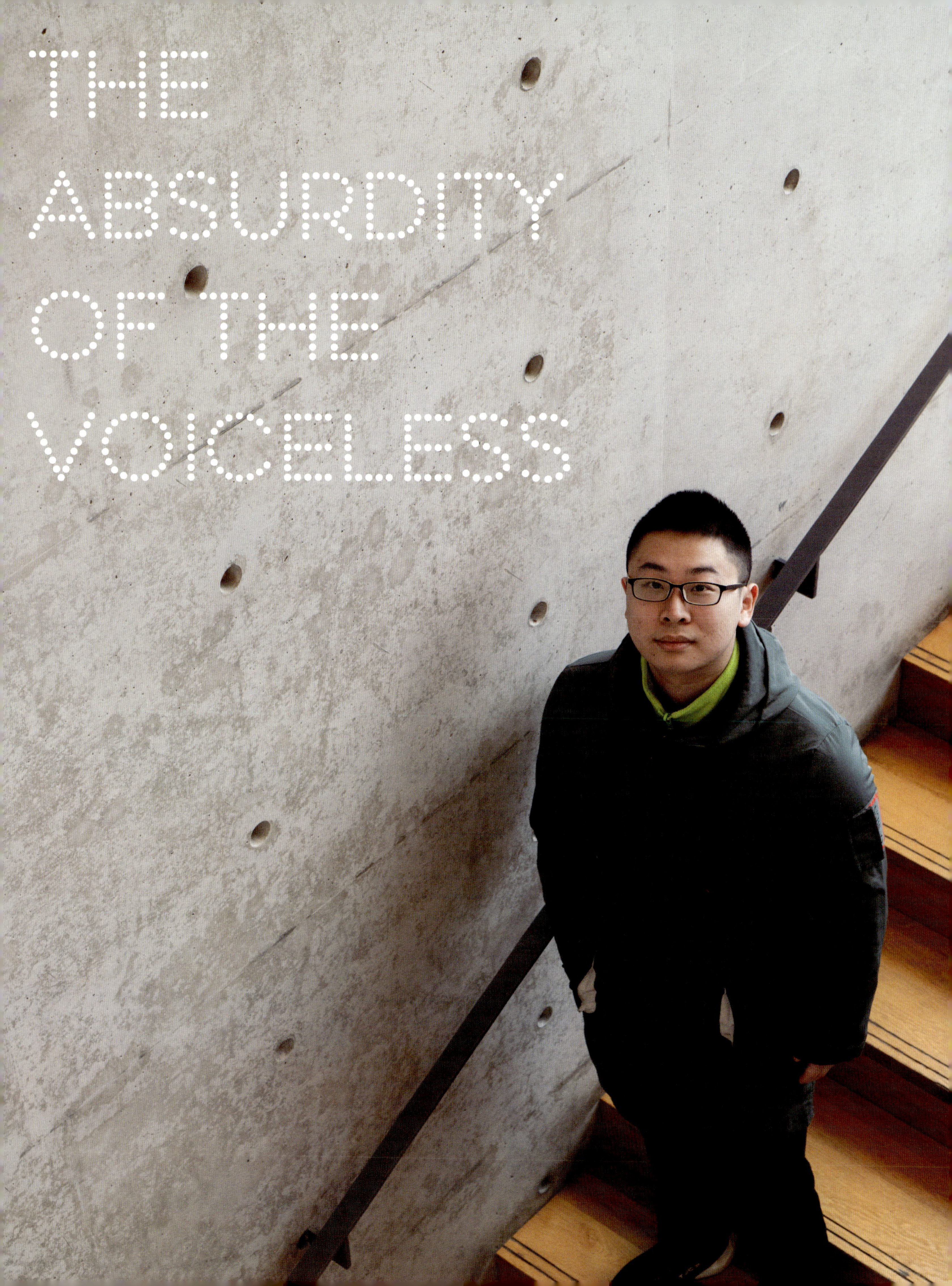

W&M At the graduation exhibition, the audience showed significant curiosity towards your artwork, displaying a keen interest in engaging with your interactive design. Was achieving this effect something you had in mind during the project's topic selection phase?

Wang Yanan We didn't anticipate such a massive turnout. When we initially picked our themes, the university required us to submit individual proposals. My concept was titled *Confronting Myself*, delving into the "mechanism of desire" of short videos. I wanted to explore why people get captivated by short videos and the technical principles behind it. As for Yixiang's proposal, *Deep Sea*, he introduced a social model called the "deep-sea dilemma", delving into the environment of those who have lost their voice, offering profound human reflections. His proposal laid the creative foundation for our graduation project.

Eventually, with the guidance of our teacher, we decided to collaborate on a piece exploring the "voiceless dilemma within short videos".

Xu Yixiang The concept of the "deep-sea dilemma" reflects my own life experience. Whether in school or in society, there's always this kind of dynamic. Let me give you an example: when choosing a student leader of a class, the candidate may not necessarily have the qualities to be a good leader. However, if a certain group of students approves him or her, others start following suit, and eventually, he or she gets elected. Those who don't agree, along with those who follow the trend, become the "voiceless", and they might not even realize this process.

When our society needs genuine feedback, the true voices of the "voiceless" gradually get overshadowed. Those who can express opinions often refrain from sharing their true thoughts, and their actions may not align with what others genuinely need. This results in an increasingly deep communication dilemma, akin to the layers of the deep sea, where the perspectives of the "voiceless" are consistently misunderstood and eventually fade away in society without anyone paying attention.

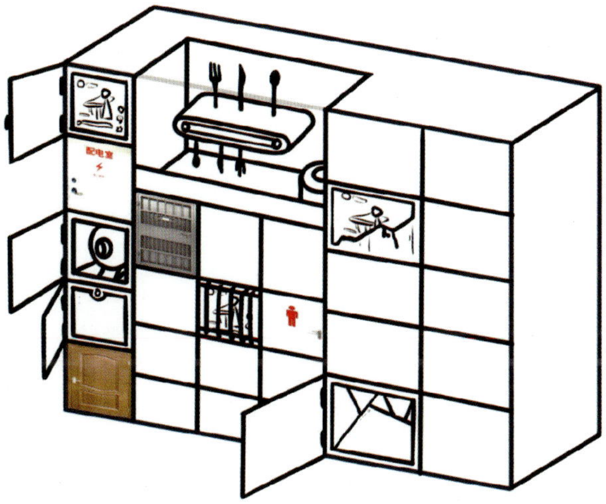

设计草图 II Sketch II

设计草图 III　Sketch III

未命名　**你们是如何把这个复杂的社会学观察视觉化的？**

王　从最初的提案，到最后的作品，我们大概迭代了七八个方案。

最初的方案是围绕一个互联网事件——“二舅治好了我的精神内耗”展开的，我们试着将它作为作品的支撑材料。另一个人物是“大衣哥”，他在互联网上爆火之后，回到村子里，村民慕名而来，围着他拍视频。无论村民拍什么，只要带上“大衣哥”的标签，就能获得非常多的流量。当时我们的思路就是去复原，或者说重新演绎这个互联网人物失语的过程。

作品的形态很像日常生活中的橱柜，有 20 个格子，每个格子里面放置一个显示屏，显示的内容有点像大衣哥的家，只不过它们来自于 20 个摄像头的监控影像。交互的主要方式就是观众拉开格子，观看橱窗背后大衣哥的具体行为。让观众扮演监视者，去模拟村民当时的状态。

W&M　How did you visualize this complex sociological observation in your work?

Wang　From the initial proposal to the final piece, we went through about seven or eight iterations.

The first concept revolved around an internet event – “My Second Uncle Cured My Mental Struggles”. We attempted to use it as the foundation for our work. Another character was the “Coat Brother”, who gained popularity on the internet and returned to his village, where villagers eagerly filmed videos around him. Regardless of what the villagers filmed, as long as it had a “Coat Brother” hashtag, it garnered a lot of traffic. Our initial idea was to reconstruct or reinterpret the process of how Internet Personalities lost their voices on the Internet.

Our work took the form of a cabinet resembling everyday life, with 20 compartments, each containing a display screen showing scenes from the Coat Brother’s home captured by 20 surveillance cameras. The main interaction involved the audience pulling open the compartments to observe the Coat Brother’s specific behaviors behind the display. We wanted the audience to play the role of observers, simulating the villagers’ state at that time.

设计草图 III　　Sketch III

未命名　**老师给这个作品什么样的反馈呢？**

王　有一位老师觉得挺好，另一位老师却不太满意。

徐　他看到我们画的图，可能觉得不是很创新，以为就是几个柜子。

王　我们跟老师交流的话，总会遇到这样一个情况，老师每周都要求出点东西，但是在这么短的时间内我们也只能想一个方案，画一些草图，没有给出很具体的效果图，然后每次都是拿着一张草图去跟老师交流，所以老师也很难听懂。特别是毕设创作前期，我们没有进入状态的时候，我们之间的交流几乎都是这样子，拿一个方案，被打掉一个。

W&M　What feedback did your teachers provide for this piece?

Wang　One teacher thought it was good, but another wasn't quite satisfied.

Xu　He saw the drawings, and he might have thought it wasn't very innovative, just a few cabinets.

Wang　When communicating with our teachers, we often encountered a situation where the teacher demanded progress every week. However, within such a short time, we could only come up with one concept, and sketch some ideas, without providing very specific visualizations. Each time, we would only bring a sketch to discuss with our teachers, so it was also challenging for our teachers to understand. Especially in the early stages of the graduation creation, when we hadn't found our rhythm, our communication was mostly like this—presenting a concept, only to have it rejected.

未命名 **你们会有特别大的情绪吗?**

王 当时倒觉得还好，可能已经麻木了，现在回想起来整个过程确实也挺失语的。一位老师会在我们已有方案的基础上调整，另一位老师可能会觉得这个方案没达到他的要求。他会给出一个很具体的参考，希望我们沿着参考作品的思路去修改。

徐 虽然推进的过程比较痛苦，但最后这个作品的风格却意外地朝着荒诞化演变。我们的创作经历和最后想要呈现的艺术效果，的确很匹配，都很荒诞。

W&M Did you experience any strong emotions during this process?

Wang At that time, it was okay. Perhaps we were already numb. Looking back, in the entire process we were quite speechless, too. One teacher might help us improve our existing concept, while another might feel our current concept doesn't meet his expectations, and he would provide specific references, hoping we would modify our approach along the lines of the reference works.

Xu Though the process was somewhat painful, the style of the final piece unexpectedly evolved towards the absurd. Our creative experience and the artistic effect we wanted to achieve turned out to be quite fitting – thiugh quite absurd.

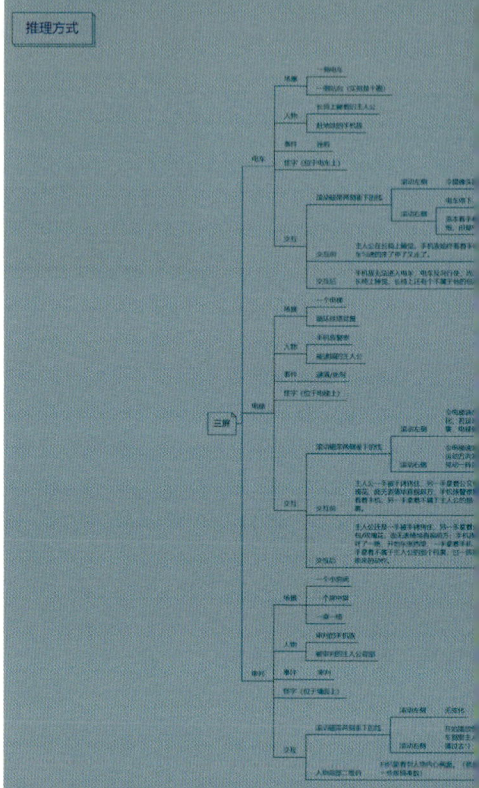

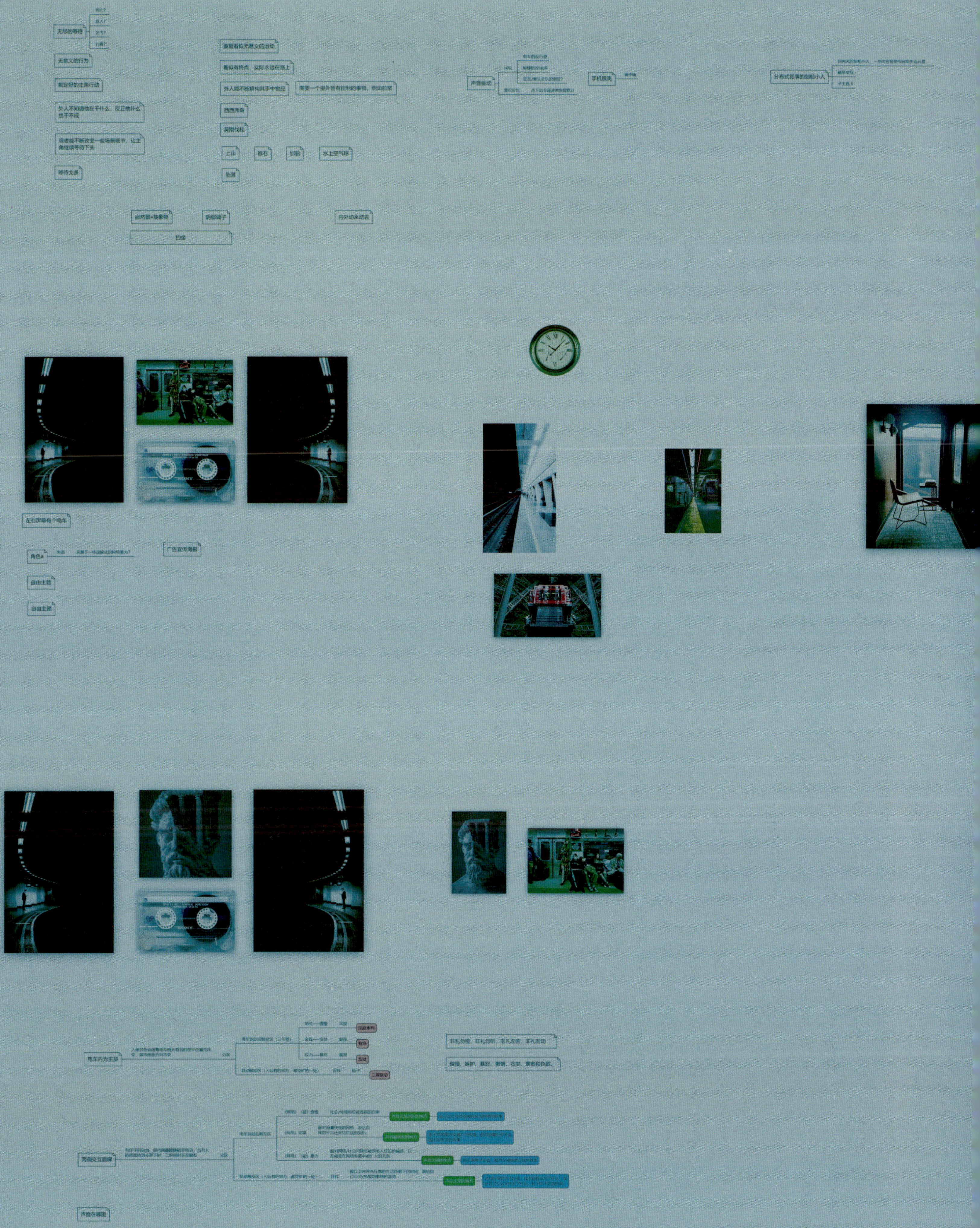
无尽的等待
无意义的行为
制定好的主角行动
外人不知道他在干什么，反正他什么也干不成
等待戈多
看似有终点，实际永远在路上
外人能不断解构其手中物品
需要一个里外皆有控制的事物，例如船桨
西西弗斯
上山
推石
划船
水上空气球
自然景+抽象物
阴郁调子
内外动来动去
钓鱼
声音驱动
手机照亮
分布式叙事的划船小人
左右屏幕有个电车
角色a
广告宣传海报
自由主题
自由主题
电车内为主屏
分区
非礼勿视、非礼勿听、非礼勿言、非礼勿动
傲慢、嫉妒、暴怒、懒惰、贪婪、暴食和色欲。
两侧交互副屏
分区
声音在哪里

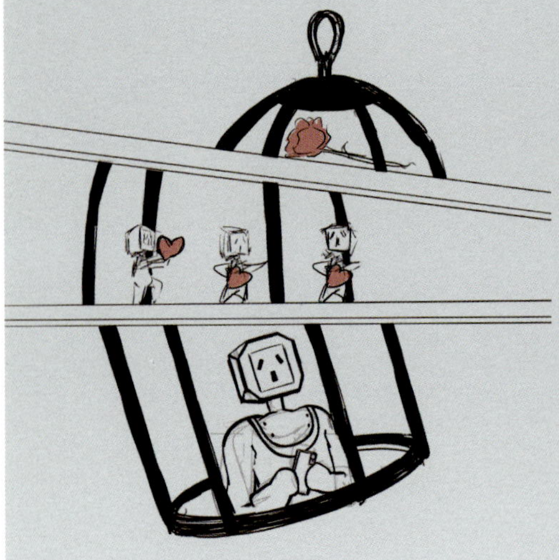

点赞情境交互影像早期草图
Sketch for the "Likes" Interactive Video

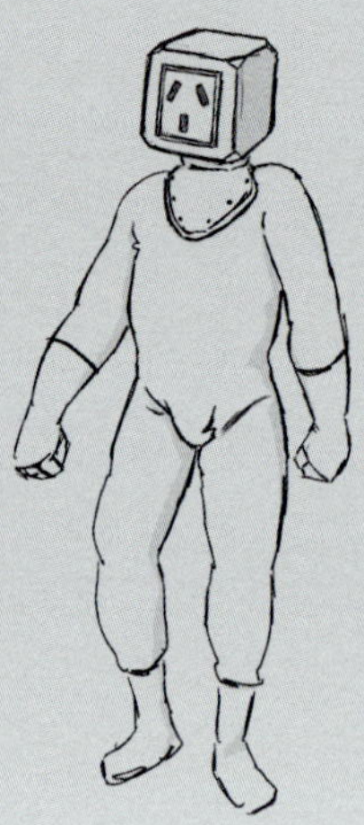

插座主人公形象草图
Sketch of the Socket-Head Character

评论情境交互影像中插电邮筒早期草图
Early Sketch of a Mailbox in the "Comments" Interactive Video

未命名　作品的形式是怎么定下来的？

徐　我们以短视频平台的的三种交互方式——“点赞、评论和转发”作为影像装置的主题，然后再根据这三个主题映射到一些日常的东西。比如说“点赞”主题，人们刷手机的时候会进入一种无意识的从众状态，非常像工厂流水线的运作。然后接着再想工厂流水线上有什么，画面里就有了履带。然后以工厂为起点，再去想哪些东西不会出现在这个空间，比如说笼子或者说笼子里面的那个人，他本身跟工厂格格不入，但是放在一起，你不会感觉到这个东西是被硬塞进去的。

“评论”主题是围绕“充气”来展开的，社交网络中“评论”的图标很像气球，我们就用了“充气”这个概念。人物造型是我们最早设置好的，就是一个插座的头部造型，有一种被榨取的感觉，正好和充气形成一种对照。

在做第三个“转发”主题的时候，时间就较赶了。我们一开始想要表达的是，个人的生活空间、工作空间以及自己的心理空间，因为不断转发而造成了空间的压缩、甚至坍塌。但是最后时间比较赶，所以我们最后把它做成了一个房间的场景，一个竖起来的房间。里面的物品以一种不稳定的状态摆放在一起，住在里边的人也跟这些物品一样，稍微施加外力，就轰然倒塌。

W&M　How was the form of the artwork determined?

Xu　We took the three interaction modes from the short video platforms – "likes, comments, and shares" – as the themes for our visual installation. We then mapped these themes to some everyday elements. For example, the "likes" theme reflects the unconscious conformity people experience when scrolling through their phones, similar to the operation of a factory assembly line. We thought about what could be on a factory assembly line, and that's how the idea of the conveyor belt emerged. Starting from the factory, we then considered what things wouldn't appear in this space, like that cage or the person inside the cage. Although they don't quite fit with the factory, when combined, you don't feel like this element was forcibly inserted.

The "comments" theme revolved around "blow up", with the icon for "comments" on social networks resembling a balloon. So, we used the concept of "blow up". The character design was one of the first things we settled on – a head shaped like a socket, conveying a feeling of being squeezed, providing a nice contrast with blow up.

When working on the third theme, "shares", time was tight. Initially, we wanted to express how continuous sharing compresses and even collapses personal living space, work space, and mental space of oneself. However, due to time constraints, we turned it into a room scene, a vertically standing room. Items inside were placed in an unstable state, and the person living there was just like those items – with just a slight external force, everything would collapse.

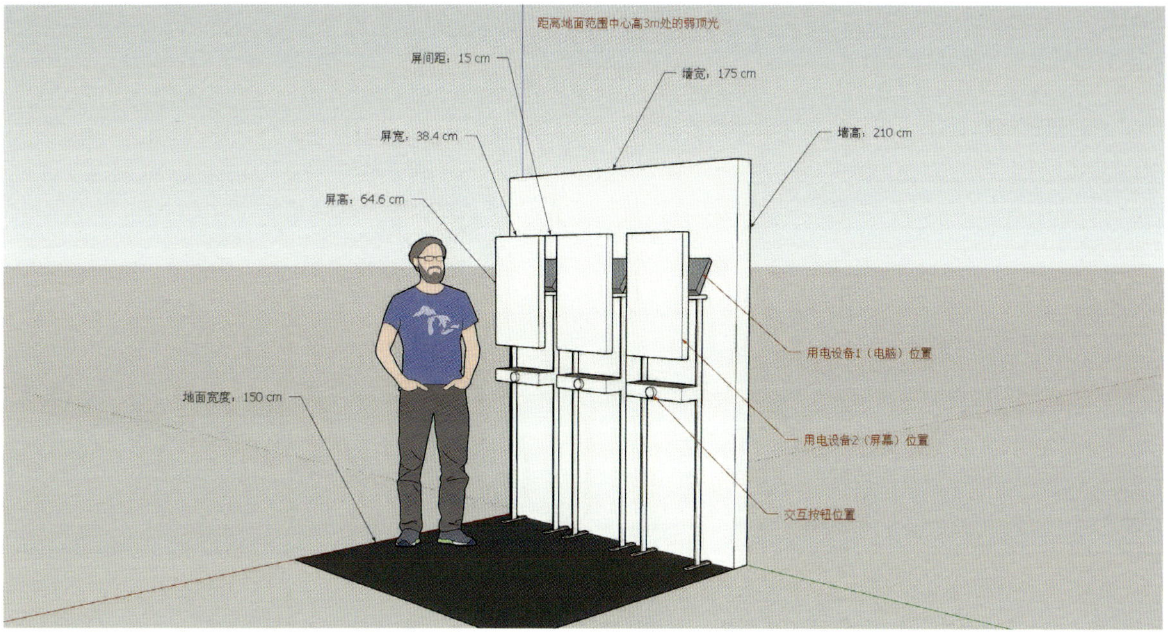

布展形式草图
Layout Sketch for the Exhibition

王 我个人比较抵触去做那种很复杂很多硬件的东西，我当时在考虑交互方式的时候，就想做傻瓜式的按钮。徐艺翔负责人物的动作设计，也是采用布娃娃系统，以极简的方式呈现。人物完全没有骨骼，像泥鳅一样。这个形象很符合失语者的形象，是一种非正常的，被外部环境摧残过的形态。

Wang I personally resist doing complex hardware-related things. When considering the interactive aspects, I wanted to create a foolproof button. Xu Yixiang was responsible for the character's motion design, he used a Ragdoll Physics to present it in a minimalist way. The character had no skeleton, like an eel. This image suited the idea of a person losing their voice – an abnormal form that has been ravaged by the external environment.

布娃娃系统技术测试
Technique Testing of the Ragdoll Physics

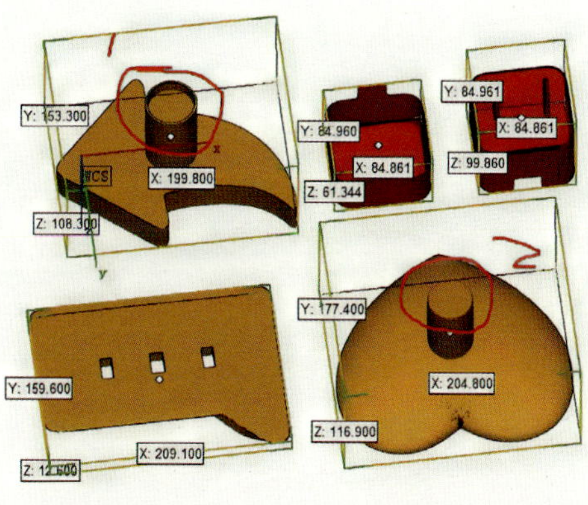

按键草图
Sketch of Buttons

评论
Comments

未命名 **这个形象曾经出现在我们日常生活中的消费场景，大商场的门口鼓风机把气球人吹得扭来扭去，它一会儿充盈，一会儿干瘪。**

徐 那时候我们的主题已经慢慢转向荒诞了。一方面我们系统查阅了很多有荒诞感的作品，另一方面我们想把互联网行为与人的状态联系在一起。第一个屏幕是对“点赞”的探讨，整个画面的布景是对现实的映射，工厂里的传送带不停的传动，上面的人被一个个弹走，很无聊也很重复，这就是短视频平台里人的状态。

后面的笼子里有一个人拿着手机不停地拍摄着自己，在永不中断的传送带上，他被分割成两半，头在上面，身子在下面。他或许以为自己是一个置身事外的人，可以嘲弄传送带上的人，但自己也像困兽一样深陷其中。

现场看展的观众通过“点赞”按钮与视频内容交互，传送带上的人会被弹下来，然后不断地堆叠在一起，像波涛一样涌动。

W&M I believe this image had previously appeared in our daily consumer scenes, where a fan at the entrance of a large mall would inflate and deflate a balloon figure, twisting and turning.

Xu Yeah, and at that time, our theme gradually shifted towards the absurd. On one hand, we extensively researched works with an absurd quality, and on the other hand, we wanted to connect internet behavior with people's states. The first screen explored the theme of “likes”, with the entire scene mirroring reality. The conveyor belt in the factory continuously moves, and people on it are bounced away one by one – it's both boring and repetitive, reflecting the state of people on those short video platforms.

In the background, there's a person inside a cage continuously filming themselves with a phone. On the never-ending conveyor belt, they are split in half, with the head above and the body below. They might think they are detached, mocking the people on the conveyor belt, but they are also trapped like a cornered beast.

At the exhibition, the audiences could interact with the video content through the “like” button. People on the conveyor belt would be bounced off and continuously stacked together, surging like waves.

《失真》现场视频
可扫码观看
Live Video of Distortion
Scan the QR Code to Watch

点赞
Likes

未命名　在你们整理查阅的荒诞风格的作品里，有没有哪位艺术家对你们的创作产生了影响？

王　勒内·玛格丽特的构图风格，的确增加了我们作品空间里的荒诞感。影像装置里的人身穿工作服，他们就是“失语者”。头部的形状是方形插座，抹去了面部特征。他们在生活中就像插座一样，被支配，被榨取。

最后一个影像装置制造了一个有关“转发”的场景。我在这部分参考了民间艺人的平衡表演，他们会把一把椅子或者一辆自行车放置在一个酒瓶上面，危机随时到来，平衡顷刻间轰然倒塌。

徐　我自己印象比较深的还有一个摄影师罗杰·巴伦，他影响了我们的布景观念。他会将一些毫不相关的物品并置在一起，产生非常荒诞的感觉，比如铁丝和鸟的尸体，还有一些雨伞之类的。我们的影像装置也是以这样的方式来组织物品之间的关系，日常生活中的东西以诡异的方式出现在三维空间中，但在这个空间，它们的出现又是合理的。

W&M　Among the absurd style works you researched and reviewed, was there any artist who influenced your creation?

Wang　The compositional style of René Magritte indeed inspired us to add a sense of absurdity to the spatiality of our work. The figures in the visual installation wear work uniforms, representing the “voiceless”. The head shape is a square socket, erasing facial features. In their lives, they are like sockets – controlled and exploited.

The final visual installation creates a scene related to “shares”. In this part, I referenced the balancing performances of street performers. They would place a chair or a bicycle on top of a bottle, giving a feeling that crisis will be imminent, and the balance would suddenly collapse.

Xu　I myself was impressed by another photographer, Roger Ballen, who influenced our idea of the set. He would juxtapose some unrelated objects to create a very absurd feeling, such as wire and bird carcasses, and some umbrellas and so on. Our visual installation also organizes the relationship between the objects in such a way that things from daily life appear in three-dimensional space in a bizarre way, but in this space, their appearance is reasonable.

未命名　在具体的创作中你们是怎么配合的？

王　在确定选题方向的前期阶段，我与艺翔都是全程保持参与。最后采纳了他提出的“深海困境”，所以在主题方面他更有主导性。我的一部分工作是去联想与这个主题相关的概念或事件。在后期的具体创作中，我负责整个场景的搭建，艺翔负责技术性的工作，涉及到代码和编程。影像装置的细节，比如布景、颜色等，是我们共同讨论的结果。

徐　我跟他之前是一个寝室，交流也比较多，所以合作起来比较顺畅，有很多该说的话都说得比较清楚，哪里有问题立刻会说出来。我有什么问题会直接跟他说，我这里不会就问他，他这里不会就会问我，互相琢磨着把作品做出来。

W&M　How did you work together in the specific creative process?

Wang　In the early stages of determining the direction of our topic, both Yixiang and I were involved throughout the whole process. In the end, we adopted his idea of the “deep sea dilemma”, so he was more in charge of the theme. Part of my job was to think of concepts or events related to the theme. In the post-production, I was responsible for the construction of the whole scene, and Yixiang was in charge of the technical work, which involved coding and programming. The details of our visual installation, such as the set and colors, are the result of our joint discussions.

Xu　We were roommates before, so there was more communication, making collaboration smoother. We clarified a lot of things clearly, and if there were any issues, we would immediately bring them up. If I had a problem, I would directly tell him, and if he had a problem, he would ask me. We figured out how to create the work together.

转发
Shares

未命名 **这三个屏幕之间有什么内在的联系吗？**

徐 在创作的过程中，的确没有想过三个屏幕合在一起会有什么特殊的含义，只能说他们在形式上是统一的，具体内容上的联系可能没有那么紧密。

王 在之前被否掉的提案中，有一个作品的屏幕之间存在联系。当时想围绕互联网人物“二舅” 做一个虚拟数字人，中间一块大屏幕，旁边四块小屏幕，强调他在病理意义上也是一个 “失语者”。他有想表达的东西，话到嘴边却支支吾吾说不出话来。主屏幕是二舅在做着想要说话的动作，旁边四个小屏是在依次叙述二舅从正常生活到最后被失语的转变过程。这五块屏幕之间是有联动的，但因为时间关系没有做下去。

W&M Is there any inherent connection between these three screens?

Xu In the creative process, we didn't really think about any special meaning when combining the three screens. It can be said that they are unified in form, but the specific content may not be so closely related.

Wang In a proposal that was rejected before, there was a connection between the screens. At that time, we wanted to create a virtual digital figure around the internet personality "Second Uncle". There was a large screen in the middle and four small screens on the sides, emphasizing that he, in a pathological sense, is also a "voiceless". He had something to express, but when it came to his mouth, he stuttered and couldn't speak. The main screen showed the Second Uncle making the motion of wanting to speak, while the four small screens sequentially narrated the transformation from his normal life to eventually becoming voiceless. These five screens were linked, but due to time constraints, we didn't proceed with it.

未命名 **毕业展览结束后，有没有一些艺术机构或者是画廊邀请你们参加展览？**

王 没有。我们不大擅长包装，也没有留一个非常好的现场视频，这个装置几乎就是一次性的。

徐 装置的零部件都在我的仓库里面放着，但不太能再组装起来了，能拆的大概都拆开了。

王 这两天把该卖的也全卖掉了。

W&M After the graduation exhibition, were there any art institutions or galleries inviting you to participate in exhibitions?

Wang No. We are not good at marketing, and there isn't a very good on-site video of our creation. This installation is almost disposable.

Xu The components of the installation are stored in my warehouse, but it's challenging to reassemble them. Most of the detachable parts have been taken apart.

Wang And in the last few days, we sold everything we could sell.

未命名　**这件作品的命运也很引人思考，它还没来得及参与到艺术品流通的环节，就已了无踪迹，似乎更增加了它的荒诞性。在作品的艺术形式和物质性实体之外，它的命运的走向也是你们作品的一部分。有一些遗憾，但又挺动人的。互联网时代里没有什么是永恒的，没有什么是一定要被每个人时刻所铭记的。**

你们觉得大众喜欢的和评论家喜欢的艺术，对你们而言差别有那么大吗？

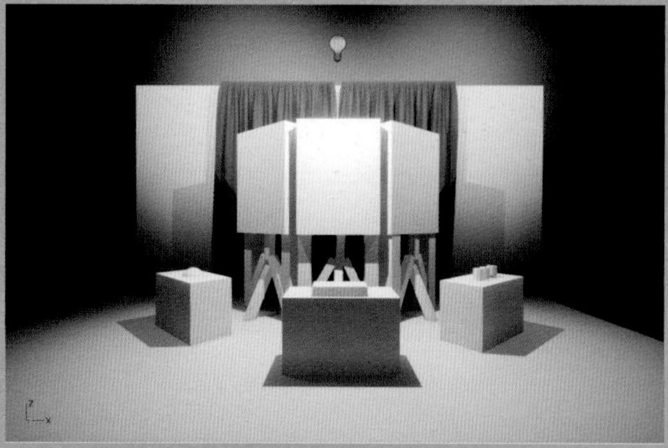

布展模拟

Simulation of the Exhibition

王　我们的这个创作还是比较接地气的，当时是6月1号开展，是儿童节，小朋友特别多，第一个点赞的按钮当时直接被敲碎了。

徐　从观众的角度看，我们的作品是比较受欢迎的，不过也有一定的运气成分在。国美教学的氛围是希望我们挖掘更深的概念，作品评价的标准也是建立在这个基础之上。当创作者都去思考什么是元宇宙，时间和精力自然偏向于概念，作品本身的接受度自然就大打折扣，这也是某种困境吧。我们俩做的作品似乎跟大家不太一样，看上去能被大众更好地接受一些。再加上来了很多小朋友，他们很喜欢那些按钮，交互的方式又比较简单，大众接受度就比较高。

我个人更喜欢看那些雅俗共赏的作品，不太想去探讨那些很遥远的，很不太实际的东西。那些东西它有讨论的必要，但就像我放一个花瓶在这里，我在花瓶上赋予了很多的概念，但是观众他只能看到这是一个花瓶，他就不想再继续去看下去。当然这只是我个人的看法，那些获奖的作品都在强调观念，我自己也很困惑。如果我继续走艺术这条路，我应该去追求那些高深的概念，还是说去沉下来做一些大家都能喜欢的，包括我自己也认可的东西。

我们这个作品是在关注失语者，他们在人群中慢慢被曲解，最后变成一个看似正常，但是无法发声的群体。我觉得我自己的状态也很像作品里所说的失语者的状态。虽然我不大能说我是一个艺术家，就拿学习艺术的这个经历来说，我和亚楠都是工科生，来到美院的时候，就会被同学或者老师贴上一个标签，我们是工科生。大家可能没有什么意见，我自己的确会有一点不舒服。在我看来，我好像就被定义成了一个纯工科生，导致我每一次在和别人合作的时候，别人就会说，你工科生，你就负责一些编程技术之类的工作。但是我离开这个学校之后，我又会被贴上一个标签，我是一个美院毕业的人。所有人看我就感觉我好像是一个很会画画的人，我就变成了一个艺科生，虽然我很喜欢画画，但是我又不是艺科生。再加上学院的氛围又是比较强调概念的，所以很多作品也都是在强调概念，做的又不是我真正喜欢的作品。只有毕业设计是我们第一次真正地从自己出发而去创作的作品。

就拿我自己来说，我就业其实也有点困难，我是等了好长时间才到一个公司里做平面设计，我自己又不是做平面设计的。你说我是艺术生吗，我其实也不是，但我又来到了这里。整个状态，包括我的人生经历，也像一个打引号的失语者一样。

一些学院派的人，他认为某个作品很有价值，概念很深。但这些作品也只是创作者拿了一个花瓶，然后给他贴了一些标签，花瓶就成了作品中的失语者。整个讨论也是很失语的状态，我也不知道怎么去解释。就像之前的“深海困境”一样，也是一层一层。其实我现在状态就是我自己既不承认我是一个工科生，我也不承认我是一个艺科生，但我好像又是从中国美术学院毕业的，我对自己的定义也开始变得很模糊。

W&M The fate of this work is also very thought-provoking. It disappeared before it could participate in the circulation of art, seemingly adding to its absurdity. Beyond the artistic form and material entity of the work, its fate is also part of your work. There are some regrets, but it's quite moving. In the internet age, nothing is eternal, and there's nothing that must be remembered by everyone at all times.

Do you feel there is a significant difference between what the general public likes and what critics appreciate in art?

Wang Our creation is relatively down to earth. It was launched on June 1st, Children's Day, and there were a lot of children. The first "like" button was directly smashed.

Xu From the audience's perspective, our work is quite popular, but luck also played a role. The atmosphere at the China Academy of Art encourages us to explore deeper conceptions, and the criteria for evaluating works are based on this foundation. When creators are all thinking about what the metaverse is, their time and energy naturally lean towards concepts, so then the acceptance of the work itself would be discounted. Our work seems to be somewhat different from others, and it appears to be more acceptable to the general public. Plus, many children joined, and they liked the buttons; the interactive method was relatively simple, so it had a high level of acceptance.

Personally, I prefer works that are widely appreciated in popular and critical circles. I don't want to delve into things that are distant from the public or impractical. Although those things may have a need for discussion, it's like me putting a vase here and assigning a lot of concepts to it, the audience can only see it as a vase; they don't want to delve further. Of course, this is just my opinion. Award-winning works always emphasize concepts. But I find it confusing. If I continue on the path of art, should I pursue profound concepts, or should I settle down and create things that everyone, including myself, will enjoy?

Our work focuses on the voiceless, who are slowly distorted in a crowd and eventually become a seemingly normal but voiceless group. I feel my own state is also like that of the voiceless in the work. Although I can't really say I'm an artist, considering my experience studying art, both Yanan and I were engineering students. When we came to the academy, we were labeled by classmates or teachers as engineering students.

People may not have any objections, but I personally feel a bit uncomfortable. In my view, I've been defined as a pure engineering student, leading to every collaboration where others say, "You're an engineering student; you should be responsible for programming and technical work." But once I leave this school, I'll be labeled as someone who graduated from an art academy. Everyone sees me as someone who's good at drawing, thus I become an art student. Even though I like drawing, I'm not a 100% art student. Plus, the atmosphere in the academy emphasizes conceptions, so many works also emphasize concepts, and they're not the kind of works I truly like. Only the graduation project was the first time we truly created something from our own perspective.

For me personally, finding a job was a bit difficult. I waited a long time before joining a company doing graphic design, even though I'm not exactly a graphic designer. Am I an art student? I'm not really, but I ended up here. My entire state, including my life experience, is like a voiceless person in quotation marks.

Some academicians believe that a certain work is very valuable, and the concept is deep. But works like this are like creators taking a vase and attaching labels to it, turning the vase into a voiceless person in the work. The whole discussion about this work is also in a very voiceless state, and I don't know how to explain it either. Like the previous "deep-sea dilemma," it's layer by layer. Actually, my current state is that I neither admit that I'm an engineering student nor an art student. I seem to have graduated from the China Academy of Art, and my self-identification has become very blurry.

邮政
开箱时间
上午 时
下午 时
筒
重金求子
18707038456

未命名　你捕捉到了你与作品之间的真正的一种互通，一种共性。

王　其实我跟艺翔观念也差不多，我在想是否有艺术壁垒这样一个问题存在。最直接的现象就是在毕业展览上很多作品，根本就看不懂。

其实很多人的创作思路存在某种“套路”，把一个很高深莫测的概念用极其华丽的外表包装起来。包装的确很重要，但体现在创作上就有点本末倒置了。

拿我们的毕设来说，我们特意设置一个最低门槛的交互，简单到小朋友都能明白。小朋友敲击按钮，影像装置里人物会有相应的动作，此时他们对这件作品的理解可能就是某种互动反馈。有参与，才会产生真正的交流。

我们不会去强迫观众理解作品的本质，不同领域的人，自然会有不同的理解。在第一个“点赞”主题里，我们加了一些彩蛋，比如当时非常火的互联网形象，有些爱冲浪的初中生就会认出来，此时他们对这件作品的理解可能就是对现实的二次表达。

最后才是作品的主旨，虽然没有很多人看出来，但或许这就是艺术，大家都在不同的维度与作品互动，呈现出多样的解读。尽管有些人一窍不通，只留下一句“好厉害”，这其实也是“失语”的一环，沉默在某种层面上也是对作品核心的一种理解。

W&M　You've captured a real connection, a commonality between you and your artwork.

Wang　Actually, my perspective aligns with Yixiang's. I wonder if there's such a thing as a barrier of art. The most direct evidence is that many artworks at the graduation exhibition are simply incomprehensible.

In reality, many creators follow a certain "routine" and wrap a profound concept in an extremely glamorous exterior. Packaging is crucial, but in terms of creation, it seems a bit inverted.

Take our graduation project, for example. We intentionally set a low threshold for our interaction installation, simple enough for even children to understand. When kids tap the buttons, the characters in the visual installation respond accordingly. At this point, their understanding of the artwork might be a form of interactive feedback. Participation leads to genuine communication.

We won't force viewers to understand the essence of the work. People from different fields will naturally have different interpretations. In the first "Like" theme, we added some Easter eggs, like the popular internet imagery at that time. Some middle schoolers who love surfing might recognize it, and their understanding of the artwork at that moment might be a secondary expression of reality.

Only at the end is the essence of the work revealed. Although not many people realize it, perhaps this is art; everyone interacts with the work on different dimensions, presenting diverse interpretations. Even for those who are clueless, leaving only a remark like "amazing" is, in essence, a part of being "mute." Silence, in a certain sense, is also an understanding of the core of our artwork.

未命名 **你们作品里的人是一种失真的状态，没有人形，没有人脸。他的情感，我在你们的作品里面阅读不到，但不代表你们是没有情感的人。但是作品本身呈现出来的状态就是这个人似乎是没有情感的，他是被抽空的一个人，他是被悬置的一个人。你们不自觉地把这种矛盾感呈现出来了，也许艺术与科技结合在一起，带来的就是一种荒诞感。**

徐 对我来说，我自己当然是很想继续做能表达我自己个人情感的东西，但是很多时间都被切割开来，很难有一颗静下来的心去思考。现实里有很多事情需要你去担心，比如说工作上的问题，生活上的问题。其实每个人都会面对这些问题，不管是普通人，还是说所谓的艺术家。只是现在这个时代都是碎片化的，都是快速阅读的状态。

我现在连自己找一会儿时间发呆去想一想，我想要干什么，可能都是一种奢侈。我就像失语者一样，有点随波逐流的感觉。但又想要在生活里找到一些东西。

王 个体的那种经历确实很重要。毕设那段时间确实是有可能成为我们人生中最后一段比较纯粹的用来创作的时间。我现在也是这个状态，我也想去创作，想去寻找一种平衡，在碎片化时间中去做创作。我不会觉得这是一个难题，其实是必须要去经历的事情，也许以后也可以把这段经历作为创作的素材。只是现实里就有一种不自知不自觉的荒诞感。

W&M The figures in your artwork represent a distorted state—no human form, no faces. I can't read their emotions in your work, but that doesn't mean you lack emotions as individuals. However, the state presented in the artwork is that these figures seem to be emotionless, drained individuals, suspended in mid-air. You unintentionally bring out this sense of contradiction; perhaps the combination of art and technology results in a kind of absurdity.

Xu For me, I certainly want to continue creating things that express my personal emotions. However, much of my time is fragmented, making it challenging to have a calm mind to contemplate. There are many things in reality to worry about, such as work-related issues and life problems. Everyone faces these issues, whether they are ordinary people or so-called artists. But in this era, everything is fragmented, in a state of rapid reading.

Even finding a little time to daydream and think about what I want to do feels like a luxury. I feel a bit like a mute person, drifting along with the tide. But I still want to find something in life.

Wang The experiences of individuals are indeed crucial. The period during our graduation project could potentially be the last relatively pure time in our lives for creating. I'm in this state now, wanting to create, seeking a balance, doing creative work in fragmented time. I don't see it as a problem; it's something that must be experienced, and perhaps I can use this experience as material for future creations. It's just that there's an unconscious sense of absurdity in reality.

《失真》展览现场

Distortion in the exhibition

The "Tendrils" of Heart

心灵的『触角』

鲍文馨：我从小生活在农村大院，父母很早就离开了家乡。童年里我时常扮演大人的角色，带着家族里的小孩在大自然里自由探索。

搬到城市之后，原来熟悉的生活环境没有了。生长在城市里的小孩，他们的习性很特别，有的害怕水，有的害怕光着脚踩在地上。我后来才知道，为了避免小孩子出现意外，有的家庭和学校在刻意营造一种“无菌”的环境。对此，我很困惑。

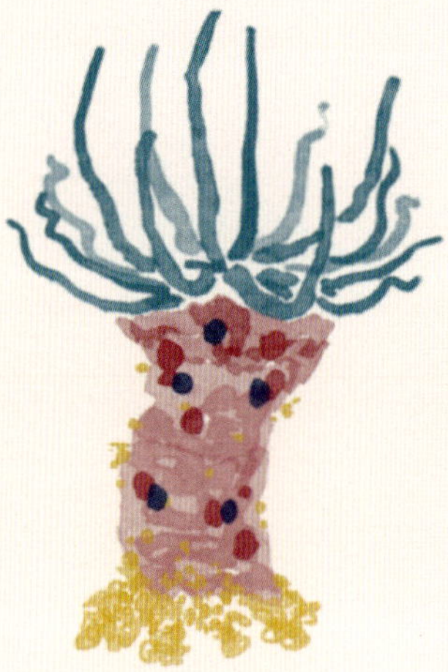

Bao Wenxin: I spent my early years in a rural courtyard as my parents left our hometown when I was very young. In my childhood, I often took on the role of an adult, exploring the great outdoors freely with other kids from the extended family.

Moving to the city changed everything. The familiar surroundings I once knew just disappeared. The urban-raised children in cities have peculiar habits; some fear water, and some are hesitant to walk barefoot on the ground. Later on, I discovered that, to prevent accidents involving children, some families and schools intentionally create a somewhat “sterile” environment. I found this perplexing.

ORIENTAL
NARRATIVE

未命名 **乡村与城市各自的生活方式塑造了儿童不同的行为模式，这应该是你毕业创作的缘起吧？**

鲍 对，做毕业创作的时候，这段经历给我带来了灵感。我读了一些临床心理学的文献，了解到有的儿童在成长期会遭遇“感觉统合失调”，简称“感统失调”。在学理上，它指的是外部的感觉刺激信号无法在儿童的大脑神经系统中进行有效的组合，使得个体无法与环境协调，久而久之就会形成心理疾病。现实中，由于家庭和学校的环境限制、过度保护等，儿童缺乏必要的运动和感知功能训练，他们的前庭平衡、触觉防御、本体感觉以及视听觉语言等多个方面就会出现障碍。

通过田野调查，针对“感统失调”我也注意到很多幼儿园的老师已经有了积极的探索。他们用按摩球、平衡触觉板等玩具，来训练儿童大脑感觉神经的灵敏度；用圆筒、平衡踩踏车、滑梯等调整前庭处理平衡和空间的能力……

这些玩具带给我很多启发，我也开始尝试用我的专业“室内纺织设计”去回应儿童的“感统失调”。一开始我想把大自然搬进室内，用纺织物制作一个大型玩具，儿童可以在这个空间里探索，互动性也很强。后来发现这么做在结构上并没有什么新意，就换了新的思路。

W&M The distinctive lifestyles of rural and urban areas surely mold the distinct behavioral patterns of children. Is this the inspiration behind your graduation project?

Bao Yes, indeed. This experience has inspired my graduation project. I delved into some literature on clinical psychology and came across “sensory integration dysfunction” that some children may experience during their developmental years. In theory, it refers to the ineffective amalgamation of external sensory stimulus signals in a child’s brain and nervous system, leading to difficulties in individual coordination with the environment and, over time, resulting in psychological issues. In reality, due to the constraints of their living environment constraints and the excessive protection from families and schools, children may lack essential training in movement and sensory functions. That leads to hindrances in various aspects such as vestibular balance, tactile defense, proprioception, and audio-visual language.

Through my field investigation later, I also noticed that many kindergarten teachers are actively exploring ways to address “sensory integration dysfunction.” They employ toys such as massage balls and balance sensory boards to enhance the sensitivity of children’s brain sensory nerves. They also use items like cylinders, balancing pedal cars, and slides to improve a child’s vestibular processing balance and spatial capabilities.

These toys sparked numerous ideas for me, and I started to leverage my expertise in “interior textile design” to respond to children’s challenges with “sensory integration dysfunction.” Initially, I intended to bring nature indoors by creating a large textile-based toy, offering children a space for exploration with strong interactivity. However, I later realized that this approach lacked novelty in structure, so I adopted a new perspective.

未命名　用你的专业去回应儿童的"感统失调"，是不是可以视为一种艺术疗愈的方式呢？

鲍　每一件艺术作品都是创作者对某种情感的表达，观众用自己的感官去接受这些信息，幸运的话，二者之间还会有强烈的感情共鸣。我想起女性主义艺术家妮基·桑法勒的一句话，大意是：艺术创作是我的归宿。我的困境，由它展现，受它启迪，因它消解。在精神层面，艺术家可以在不借助药物的情况下，通过艺术创作完成自我疗愈，欣赏艺术的人也会有这样的体验吧！

W&M　Can using your expertise to address children's "sensory integration dysfunction" be considered a form of art therapy?

Bao　Every piece of artwork is an expression of the creator's emotions. Audiences can engage with this information through their senses, and if fortunate, a strong emotional resonance could happen between the two. I can recall a quote from feminist artist Niki de Saint Phalle (1930-2002): Art-making is a way of finding myself and losing myself; My struggles are revealed through it, inspired by it, and dissolved by it. On a spiritual level, I think artists can achieve self-healing through artistic creation without relying on drugs, and those who appreciate art may also share in this experience!

未命名　具体到创作上，《绒鳞》的结构是如何确定下来的？

鲍　大学课堂上有位老师曾经带着我们用显微镜观察自然，我后来也买了蝴蝶标本。显微镜的放大功能让我看到了蝶翅的微观结构，它颜色绚丽，几何图形规律地排列在一起。不过，我需要用设计语言去转化自然的形态。事实证明这个设计思路是对的，所以过程还蛮顺利，大方向上没有改动，剩下的就是不停地扩展它的细节。

W&M　Regarding your creation, how did you finally determine the structure of *Velvet Scales*?

Bao　In my college, a teacher once guided us to observe nature through a microscope, and I also purchased a butterfly specimen myself later. The magnification of the microscope allowed me to see the intricate structure of butterfly wings, with vibrant colors arranged in geometric patterns. However, I had to translate this natural form using design language. This design approach turned out to be effective, so my creative process went quite smoothly. The general direction of my design remained unchanged, and the rest involved continually expanding on its details.

未命名　**《绒鳞》在视觉上有着海洋生物的特质，您有什么特殊的用意吗？**

鲍　我的家乡是一个典型的内陆城市，所以一直以来我都很向往海洋。它有着独特且完整的生态系统，很漂亮，也很缤纷。对我来说，海洋是一个充满想象力的空间。《绒鳞》系列的四件作品分别用了水母、章鱼、海葵、珊瑚的造型。水母飘逸舒展的造型令我着迷，后来我把它作为《绒鳞》的主造型。原本计划把它吊在空中，但场地并不支持，就没有实现展览效果。不过，毕业展览期间有小孩非常感兴趣，他们会上前摸一摸碰一碰，我觉得我想要的效果也达到了。

W&M　Your *Velvet Scales* visually incorporates characteristics of marine life. Do you have any specific intentions behind this?

Bao　My hometown is a typical inland city, so I have always held a fascination for the ocean. The ocean has a unique and complete ecosystem, beautiful and colorful. For me, the sea is a space full of imagination. The four pieces in the *Velvet Scales* series feature shapes inspired by jellyfish, octopus, sea anemones, and coral. I was captivated by the graceful and expansive form of the jellyfish, and later it led me to choose it as the main form for *Velvet Scales*. Originally, I planned to suspend it in the air, but the venue I planned to place it in did not support this, so my intended exhibition effect couldn't be realized. However, during our graduation exhibition, children, they would come forward to touch and feel. I felt that my intended effect was still achieved.

《绒鳞》草图

Sketch of Velvet Scales

《绒鳞》
Velvet Scales

未命名 **那一刻你有什么感觉？**

鲍 很有满足感。我的创意能在现实中得到认可，让我感到非常踏实。有的时候就怕自己做的东西太虚，有的时候也怕太接地气。

W&M How did you feel at that moment?

Bao I felt a deep sense of satisfaction. It's reassuring to see my creativity being acknowledged in the real world. Sometimes I worry that what I create might be too abstract, and other times, I fear it's too grounded.

未命名 **您是如何实现作品的触觉感的？**

鲍 除去纤维类的材料，我其实也尝试过诸如塑料、硅胶、滴胶等其他新兴材料。但如果花费太多时间在材料选择上，问题就会变得复杂，因为可选择的种类实在太庞杂了，不能看到什么就用什么。我需要将材料统一在造型设计中。

W&M How did you achieve the tactile element in your work?

Bao Besides using fiber materials, I also experimented with other emerging materials like plastic, silicone, and droplet glue. However, delving too much into material selection can be complicated due to the overwhelming options available. Choosing based on appearance alone isn't practical. I needed to unify the materials in the design.

《绒鳞》局部 I
Detail of *Velvet Scales* I

未命名　在这个过程中有没有艺术家对你的创作产生影响？

鲍　前期我看了大量的作品，每一件都给我留下了很深的印象。比如伊娃·法布雷加斯的《纠结》，这是一件综合了雕塑、视频与声音的软雕塑。作品的媒介材料是感官球和莱卡（一种人造弹性纤维品牌），它的造型像互相缠绕的肠道，可以通过触碰发出声音并随之震动，就像我们隆隆作响的肚子一样。这件作品在"新冠病毒"肆虐全球的时期展出，伊娃想要告诉我们，人类肠道内的益生菌与有害菌群是一种共生的状态，也许我们的未来也会跟病毒继续共生下去。除此之外，伊娃称它们为"触觉声音乐器"，通过触觉与听觉，观众可以与艺术链接在一起。这种艺术疗愈的观念很启发我。

还有英国工业艺术家夏洛特·金斯诺斯《嘿！繁殖椅子》，伊朗裔加拿大艺术家霍达·扎尔巴夫的旧物改造的纤维装置，等等。

回到我自己的创作，我只能从我的生活出发去选择我擅长的材料，不管是造型还是颜色，它们都带着我深刻的个人印记，是属于我自己的表达。

W&M　Did any artists influence your creation during this process?

Bao　In the beginning, I explored many works, and each left a deep impression on me. For example, Eva Fàbregas's *Tangles* (2020), which is a soft sculpture that combines sculpture, video, and sound. The materials used in it include sensory balls and Lycra (a brand of synthetic elastic fiber). The sculpture resembles intertwined intestines, producing sound and vibration when touched, like the rumbling of our stomachs. This work was displayed during the global spread of Covid-19, and what Eva wanted to convey was that the symbolic relationship between beneficial and harmful bacteria in the human intestines mirrors our potential future coexistence with viruses. She refers to them as "tactile sound instruments," connecting the audience with art through touch and hearing. And this reflects the concept of art therapy, which inspires me a lot.

Additionally, works like Charlotte Kingsnorth's *Hi!breed chairs* (2021) and Honda Zarbaf's fiber installations transformed from old objects also had influences on my work.

But as I returned to create my own work, I had to choose materials based on my life. Whether in terms of form or color, they carry profound personal imprints that belong to my expression.

未命名 **《绒鳞》的配色让人非常放松，让人与海洋产生了有机的连接。**

鲍 《绒鳞》的色彩非常缤纷，是因为我大胆地尝试了并不擅长的黄紫色调，它们是我从海洋生物纹路斑点上提取的颜色。虽然我个人比较喜欢莫兰迪灰色调，但用饱和度高的黄色、紫色和棕色来呈现触角的质感，反而让我的创作在视觉观感上更为和谐。所以，大自然才是最好的老师。

W&M The color scheme of *Velvet Scales* is indeed very relaxing, and I guess that could create an organic connection with the ocean for audiences.

Bao The colors in *Velvet Scales* are vibrant because I boldly experimented with hues like yellow and purple, which I'm not typically good at. These colors were extracted from the patterns and spots of marine creatures. While I personally prefer Morandi gray tones, I think using highly saturated yellow, purple, and brown to present the texture of the tentacles just visually harmonized my creation. Nature is indeed the best teacher.

《绒鳞》草图

The Sketch of *Velvet Scales*

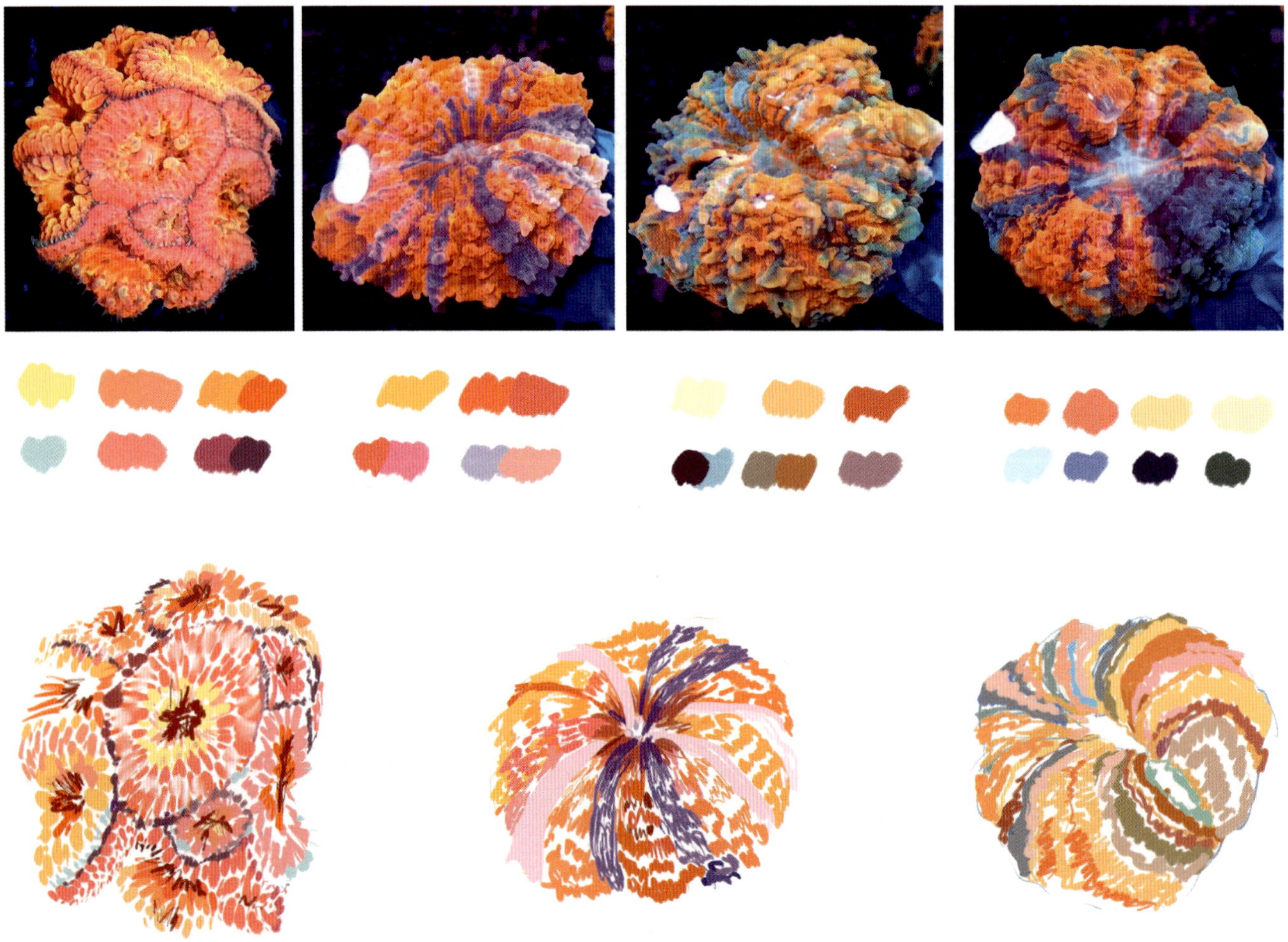

《绒鳞》局部 II
Detail of *Velvet Scales* II

未命名 **在设计好造型，搭配好颜色之后，《绒鳞》手工的部分是如何完成的？**

鲍 我画完草图后，确定好每个小区域我想表达的效果，每个部位都有代号。其中手工需求最多的部分就是鳞片，我用通俗易懂的名字“棉花耳朵”和工人沟通，确定好方案后由工厂的生产线批量制作，机器完成切割、绣花、充棉之后，我需要将它们一个个粘上去，慢慢完成它的造型。

其实最初的颜色设计与最后用的材料还是有出入的，只能去市场去挑选最符合作品色调的织物，最终的成品效果还算是蛮惊喜的。

W&M After designing the shape and coordinating the colors, how did you complete the manual part of your *Velvet Scales*?

Bao After sketching, I outlined the effects I wanted for each smaller part, assigning a code to each of them. The most labor-intensive part was the scales. I communicated my design plan with the workers using a straightforward name “cotton ears”. Once the factory’s production line mass-produced them, including machine processes like cutting, embroidery, and filling cotton, I had to stick them on one by one to gradually shape my creation.

In fact, the final color of the produced materials deviated from my initial design, so I had to choose fabrics in the market that best matched the tone of the artwork. However, the result was quite surprising.

未命名：相比于传统的架上绘画，《绒鳞》的创作多了一层与工业生产和消费市场打交道的过程，你是如何适应的？

鲍 我所学的专业本身就需要融合市场、参与到工业生产的环节中，不是传统艺术家的单打独斗。我们负责设计构想，工厂负责工艺流程。但双方沟通起来可能“驴头不对马嘴”，我纠结的是颜色是造型，他强调技术与现实。为了最大程度上还原效果图，我需要在现场不断跟工人协调，这个过程非常消耗。经历过这些之后，我觉得自己随时可以在工厂的任何岗位上班，已然熟练掌握每一门技术了。（笑）

W&M So compared to traditional easel painting, the creation of your *Velvet Scales* involves an additional process that deal with industrial production and the consumer market. How did you adapt to this?

Bao Unlike the traditional artists who tend to work alone, my major itself requires integrating with the market and participating in the industrial production process. We're responsible for giving the design while factories handle the craft process. However, communication between us can sometimes be challenging because we may not see eye to eye on certain aspects. I struggled with the emphasis on color and form while they focused on technicalities and practicality. To recreate the visual effect as accurately as possible, I had to coordinate continuously with the workers on-site, which was very consuming. After going through all this, I feel like I could work in any position at the factory at any time because I have become proficient in every technique. Haha.

未命名 你是怎么找到源头工厂的？

鲍 过程其实蛮曲折的。一开始我是通过设计自己喜欢的玩偶来寻找制作工厂，结果由于经验不足，吃了很多亏。制作报价、产品质量、物流服务都存在问题，后来又陆续考察了十几个工厂，最终和扬州的一家公司达成了合作。虽然他们之前没有做过非常精细的产品，但解决问题的方式让我看到了合作的希望。

W&M How did you find the original factory?

Bao The process was quite complicated. Initially, I sought production factories that design dolls I liked, but due to lack of experience, I faced numerous setbacks. Issues with production quotes, product quality, and logistics services arose. Later, I visited over a dozen factories, eventually partnering with a company in Yangzhou. While they hadn't previously dealt with very refined products like this, their problem-solving approach gave me hope for collaboration.

未命名 这些困难都是你一个人克服的吗？

鲍 是的。

W&M Did you overcome these difficulties on your own?

Bao Yes.

未命名　老师会有帮助吗？

鲍　老师其实不了解我在做什么，不过他们鼓励我们去社会上历练。毕业之后，我的一部分精力放在了设计 ACG 文化的衍生品。去跟工厂打交道的过程，让我看到了更多的可能。

W&M　Did your supervisors offer any help?

Bao　Actually, my supervisors didn't understand what I was doing, but they encourage us to gain experience in society. After graduation, part of my energy went into designing derivative products in the ACG subculture. Dealing with factories allowed me to see more possibilities.

未命名　市场会对你有诱惑吗，它会不会让你与艺术之间的距离变得遥远？

鲍　的确很纠结，因为一旦接触衍生品的领域，我的设计思路也会被它影响。不过我并没有焦虑，因为我在做擅长的事情，并且活在当下。

我觉得今天这个时代对艺术家还是很友好的，人们更在意精神上的满足，艺术家的创意也有了用武之地。当这些作品出现在艺术市场上，人们会被它们的多元设计和文化表达而吸引，获得一种精神上的疗愈。

W&M　Is the market tempting for you, or does it distance you from art?

Bao　Indeed, it's a dilemma because once involved in the field of derivative products, my ways of thinking about designs can be influenced by it. However, I'm not anxious about it because I'm doing what I'm good at and living in the present.

I feel this era is still artist-friendly; people care more about spiritual satisfaction, and artists' creativity can therefore find its place. When these works from those artists appear in the art market, people are attracted to their diverse designs and cultural expressions, experiencing a kind of spiritual healing.

未命名　未来你还会以毕业作品的方式去做创作吗？

鲍　我觉得很难了。我现在的时间和精力更多地放在了与市场接触，很难再有类似毕业设计的这种舞台了。在那里，我可以天马行空，可以放肆地表达我想要的艺术。不过我也并没有放弃，有了更多的实践锻炼和生活积累，对未来的艺术创作也是好事。来日方长。

W&M　Will you continue to create in the form of your graduation projects in the future?

Bao　It's challenging. Currently, my time and energy are more focused on engaging with the market, making it difficult to find a stage similar to the graduation design where I could freely express my artistic ideas. However, I haven't given up. With more practical experience and life accumulation, it's a good thing for future artistic creations. The future is long.

Chatting with Dürer: On Artificial Intelligence

与丢勒讨论人工智能

未命名 **过去一年，“人工智能”从少数科学家的研究，迅速演变成一个大众话题。你是从什么时候开始关注它与艺术之间的可能性的，之前有做过相关的作品吗？**

张少语 我本硕学的都是版画专业，但人工智能和科技美学一直是我的兴趣。读本科的时候，我就关注到了一些先锋艺术家，他们的作品有很多都采用了计算机或其他新兴媒介（比如太空、生物材料），人工智能也是其中之一。

硕士一年级，我第一次尝试用人工智能创作作品，主题与西湖、月球有关，使用的技术是CycleGAN 生成对抗网络模型。这个技术是我当时能接触到的最大众化的人工智能算法，从本地部署环境、修改代码、做数据集，到最终生成作品，整个创作过程出现了非常多的问题。还好有一位在互联网公司工作的软件工程师不吝赐教，在他的指点下，才磕磕绊绊地完成了第一次创作。

这次创作之所以关注月球和西湖，与我的生活环境有关。中国美术学院南山校区距离西湖只有五十米，工作之余，总会和朋友在西湖边漫步休息。凌晨的西湖很平静，甚至是寂静的，偶尔能看到月球的影子倒映在湖面。在那个时刻，我会幻想自己身处在陨石坑之中，西湖变得干涸，没有人，没有水，没有生命。后来，我尝试用风格迁移的技术，将地球上的西湖图像转换为月球陨石坑的样子。与此同时，程序指令还可以生成“月球陨石坑转化为西湖”的图像。我当时的想法很简单，就是想让观众既可以坐在西湖边感受月球坑，又可以幻想在月球上欣赏“西湖水”。

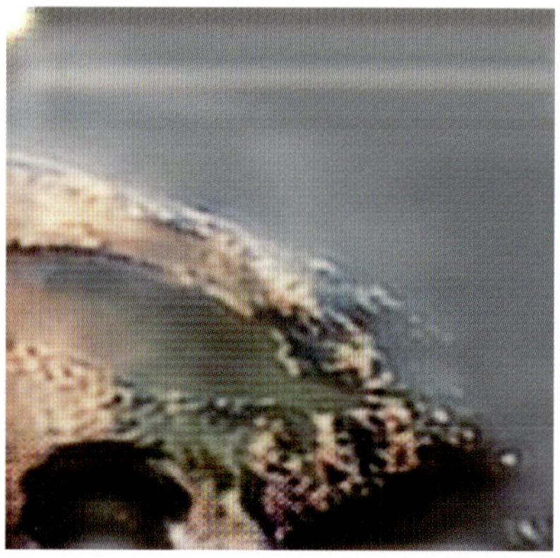

W&M In the past year, artificial intelligence has rapidly evolved from the research of a few scientists into a mainstream topic. When did you start paying attention to its possibilities in art, and have you created any relevant works before?

Zhang Shaoyu I majored in printmaking for both my undergraduate and graduate studies, but artificial intelligence and the aesthetics of technology have always been my interests. During my undergraduate years, I paid attention to some avant-garde artists. Many of their works employed computers or other emerging media (such as space and biological materials), and artificial intelligence was one of them.

In the first year of my master's program, I made my first attempt to create works using artificial intelligence. The theme of my work was related to the West Lake and the moon, and the technology I used was the CycleGAN generative adversarial network model. This technology was the most popular artificial intelligence algorithm I could access at that time. The entire creative process, from setting up a local deployment environment, modifying code, creating datasets to generating the final artwork, was filled with many challenges. I was fortunate that a software engineer working in an internet company generously guided me, and with his help, I completed the first creation with some stumbling.

Picking the moon and West Lake for this creation was all about the living environment around me. After work, I'd often wander along West Lake with my friends. The predawn hours turned West Lake into a serene, almost silent scene. And every now and then, I can catch the reflection of the moon upon the surface of the lake. It was during these moments that I'd imagine being in a lunar crater, with West Lake all dried up, no people, no water, and no life. Later on, I tried using style transfer technology to morph images of West Lake on Earth into a lunar crater on the Moon. At the same time, I could also use the program instructions to generate an image of "Moon crater transformed into West Lake." My idea back then was straightforward—I wanted the audience to sit by West Lake, feeling the lunar vibes, while also daydreaming about enjoying the "West Lake" on the Moon.

MOON

月球

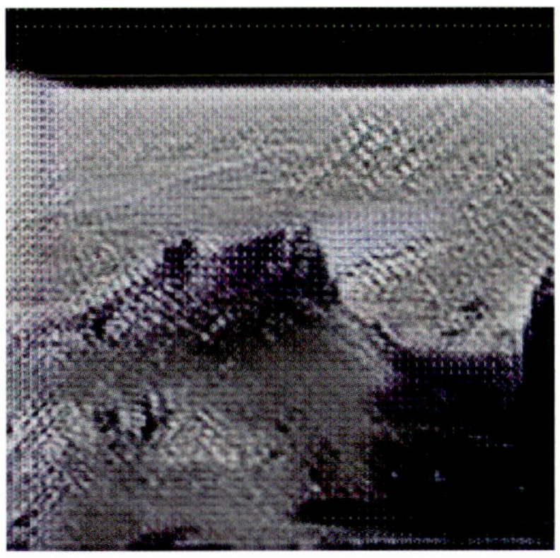

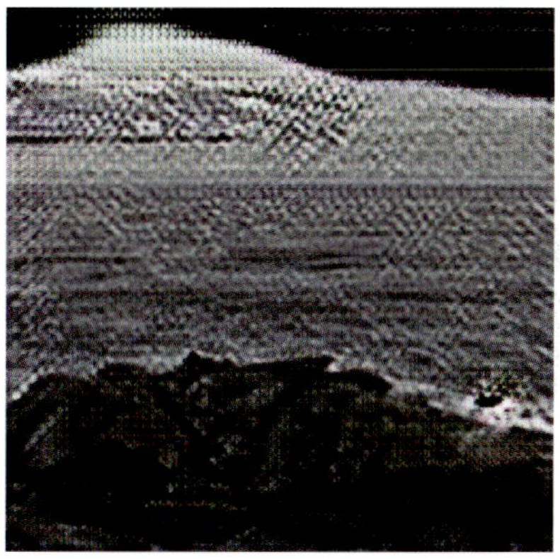

WEST LAKE

西湖

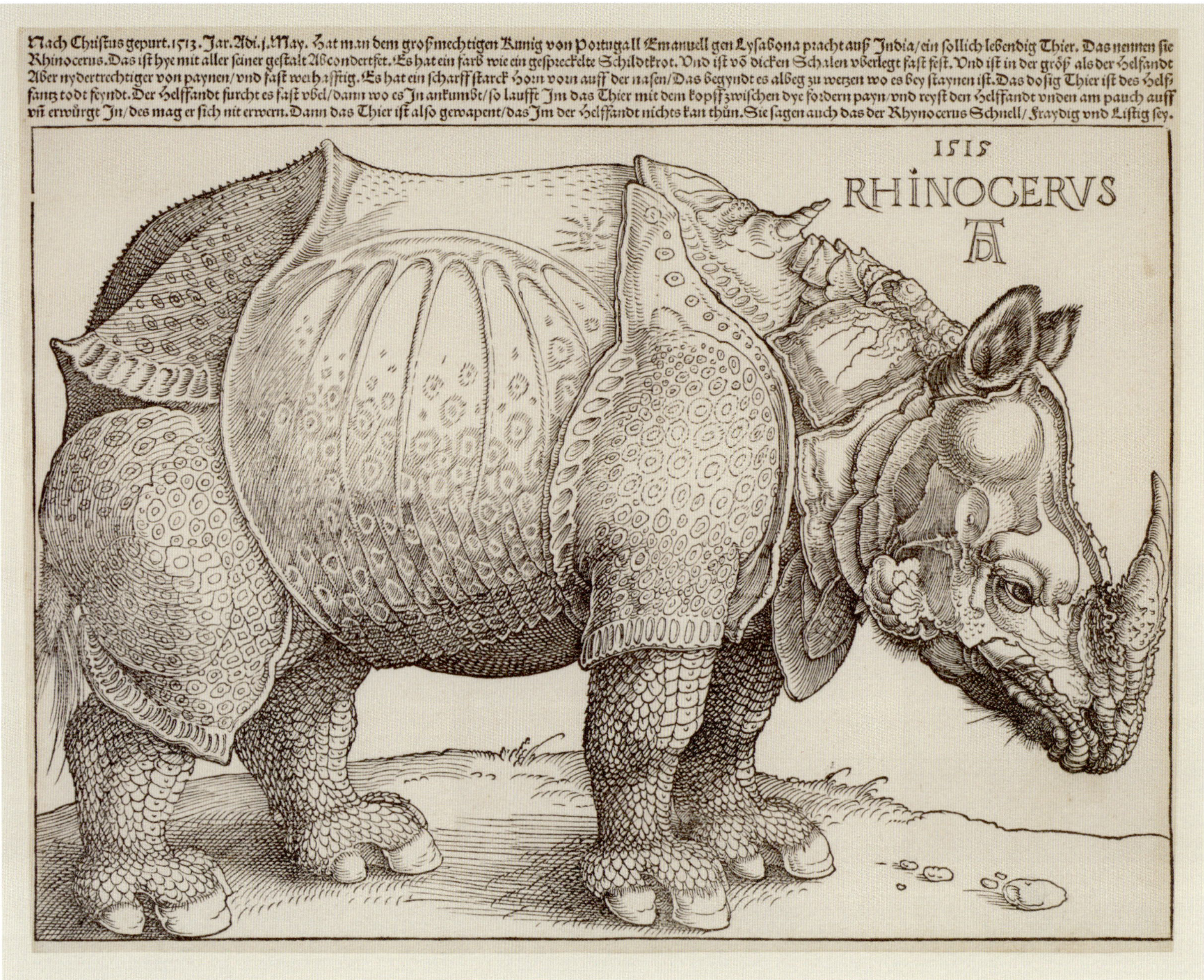

《犀牛》
阿尔布雷特·丢勒

The Rhinoceros
Albrecht Dürer

艺术史中的犀牛

The rhino in art history

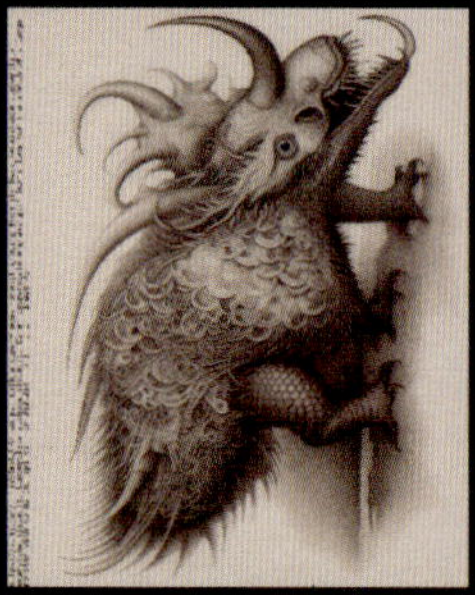

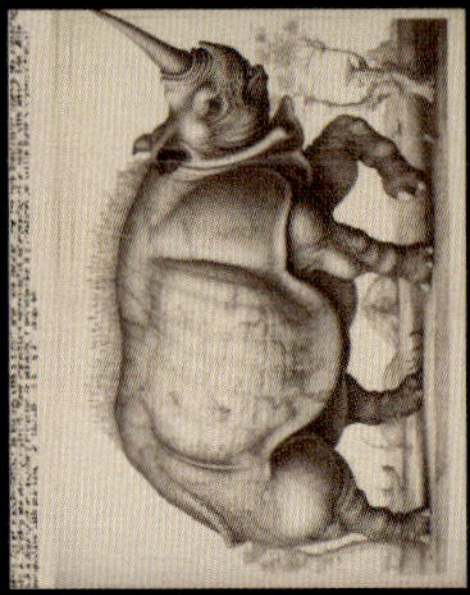

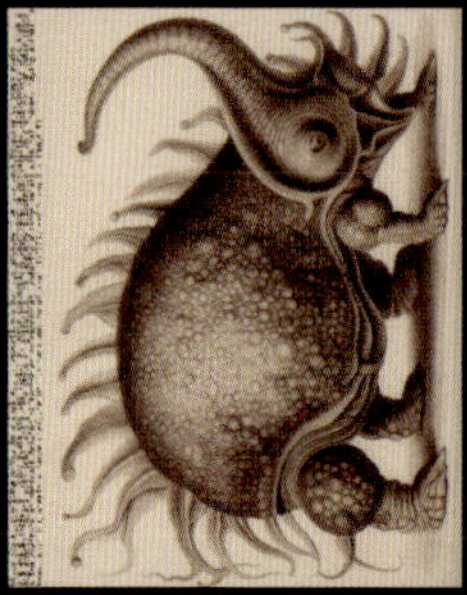

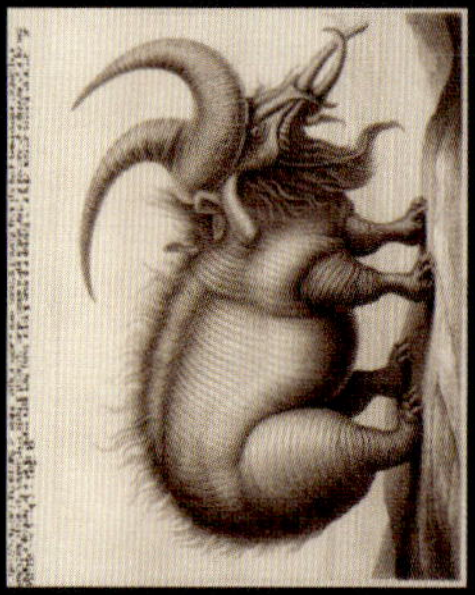

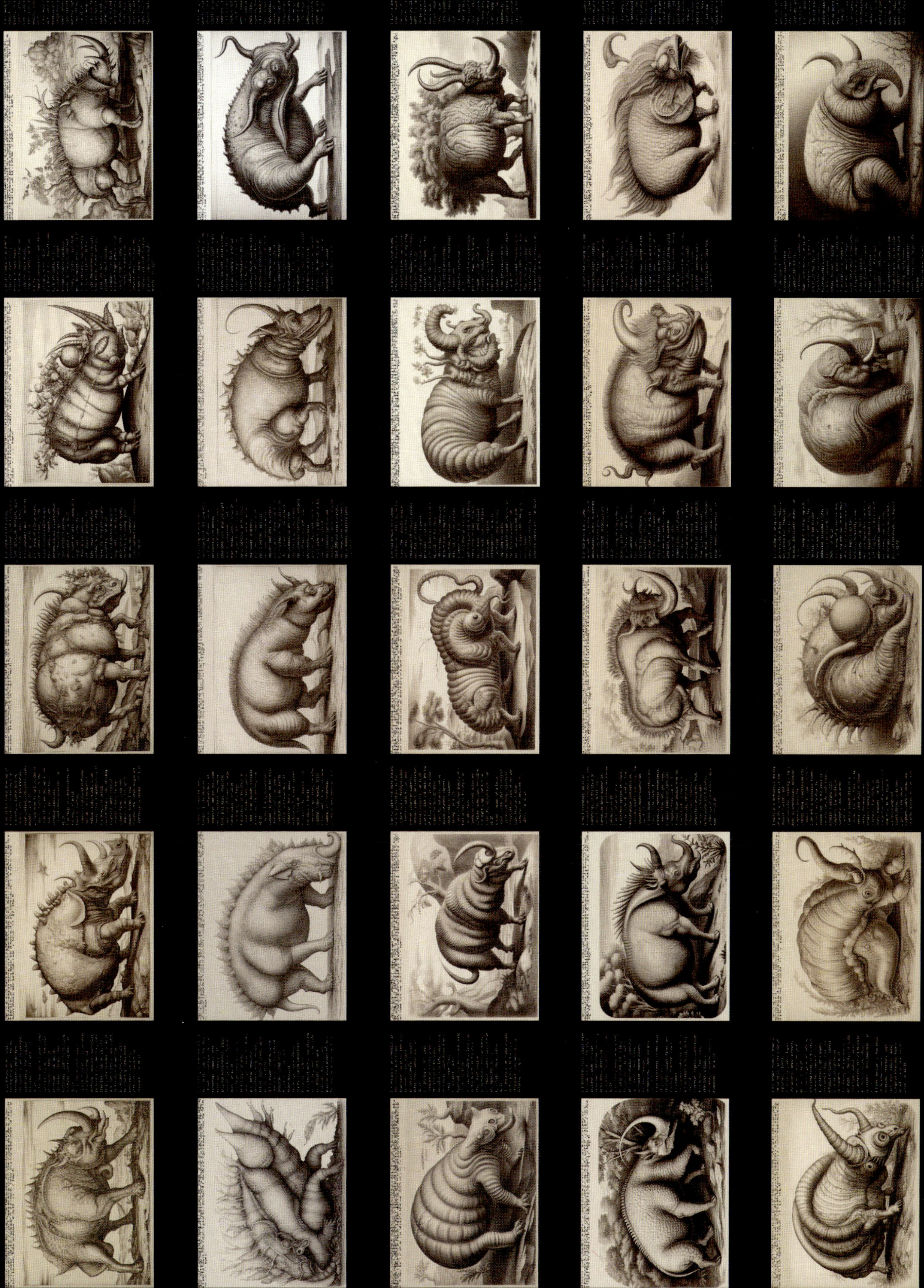

未命名 **为什么选择用丢勒的版画作为毕业作品的创作主题?**

张 在学校的一次课程作业上，我曾经把文艺复兴时期的德国版画家丢勒当作我的研究对象。阅读文献的过程，让我对丢勒的《犀牛》产生了浓厚的兴趣。2023 年，当生成式人工智能，如 ChatGPT、Midjourney、Stable Diffusion 等软件开始流行，丢勒的那只犀牛再度出现在我的脑海。

为了做好这件作品，我尽可能地翻阅、梳理有关丢勒的《犀牛》的研究资料，前期准备花了很长时间。真正进入图像制作环节的时候，毕业展览已经临近了。我在 20 天高强度的工作下，完成了这件作品。

丢勒的《犀牛》的灵感源于一幅由不知名画家所画的素描印度犀牛，在我看来，它与人工智能制作的图像有相似性。这只犀牛形象很怪异，全身长满鳞片，鼻子上长着锋利的独角，脊椎上凸起硬角、硕大的脚趾宛如大象一般。如果今天的艺术家想用 AI 来制作犀牛图像，必须像丢勒当年一样，输入类似“长得跟大象一样”、“有很多鳞片”的关键词。如果直接输入“犀牛”，算法选择出来的就会是自然界里的犀牛。

通过一张图和关键词来生成图像，这是 AI 绘画的一种工作模式。在艺术史上，丢勒的木刻版画在接下来的几个世纪里被不断复制和再创作，他们都是在跟丢勒对话。而在今天的互联网上，人们讨论着人工智能生成图像的版权、开源社区里的算法模型。过去与现在交织在一起，有某种深刻的共通性。

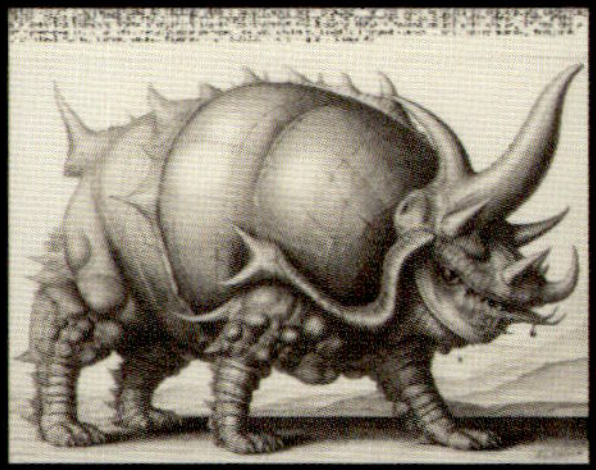

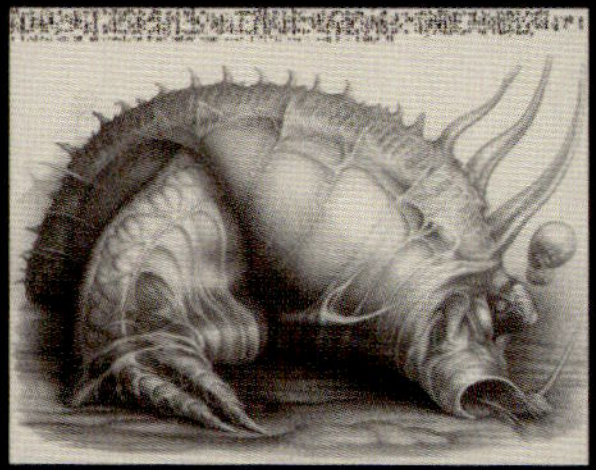

W&M Why did you pick Dürer's prints as the theme for your graduation work?

Zhang During a school assignment, I once chose the German printmaker Dürer from the Renaissance period as my research subject. As I delved into research and literature reading, his piece *Rhinoceros* caught my eye. Fast forward to 2023, with the rise of generative AI, especially technologies like ChatGPT, Midjourney, Stable Diffusion, Dürer's rhinoceros made a comeback in my mind.

When I started working on this project, I spent a considerable amount of time researching everything related to Dürer's *Rhinoceros*. By the time I got to the image creation phase, the deadline for the graduation exhibition was just around the corner. Despite the tight schedule, I completed this work.

Dürer's inspiration for *Rhinoceros* came from a sketch of an Indian rhinoceros drawn by an unknown artist, and to me, it shares similarities with the images produced by artificial intelligence. The rhinoceros is peculiar, covered in scales, with a sharp horn on its nose, prominent hard angles on its spine, and elephant-like large toes. Simply entering "rhinoceros" would result in the algorithm choosing an image of a rhinoceros from the natural world.

This is a working mode of AI painting, it creates images by blending a single picture and some keywords into a mix. In art history, Dürer's woodcut prints have been continuously replicated and reinterpreted for centuries. Essentially, they're engaging in a dialogue with Dürer. Today, there are ongoing discussions about copyright issues related to AI-generated images and the algorithms used in open-source communities on the Internet. The present echoes the past, to some extent revealing a profound commonality between the two.

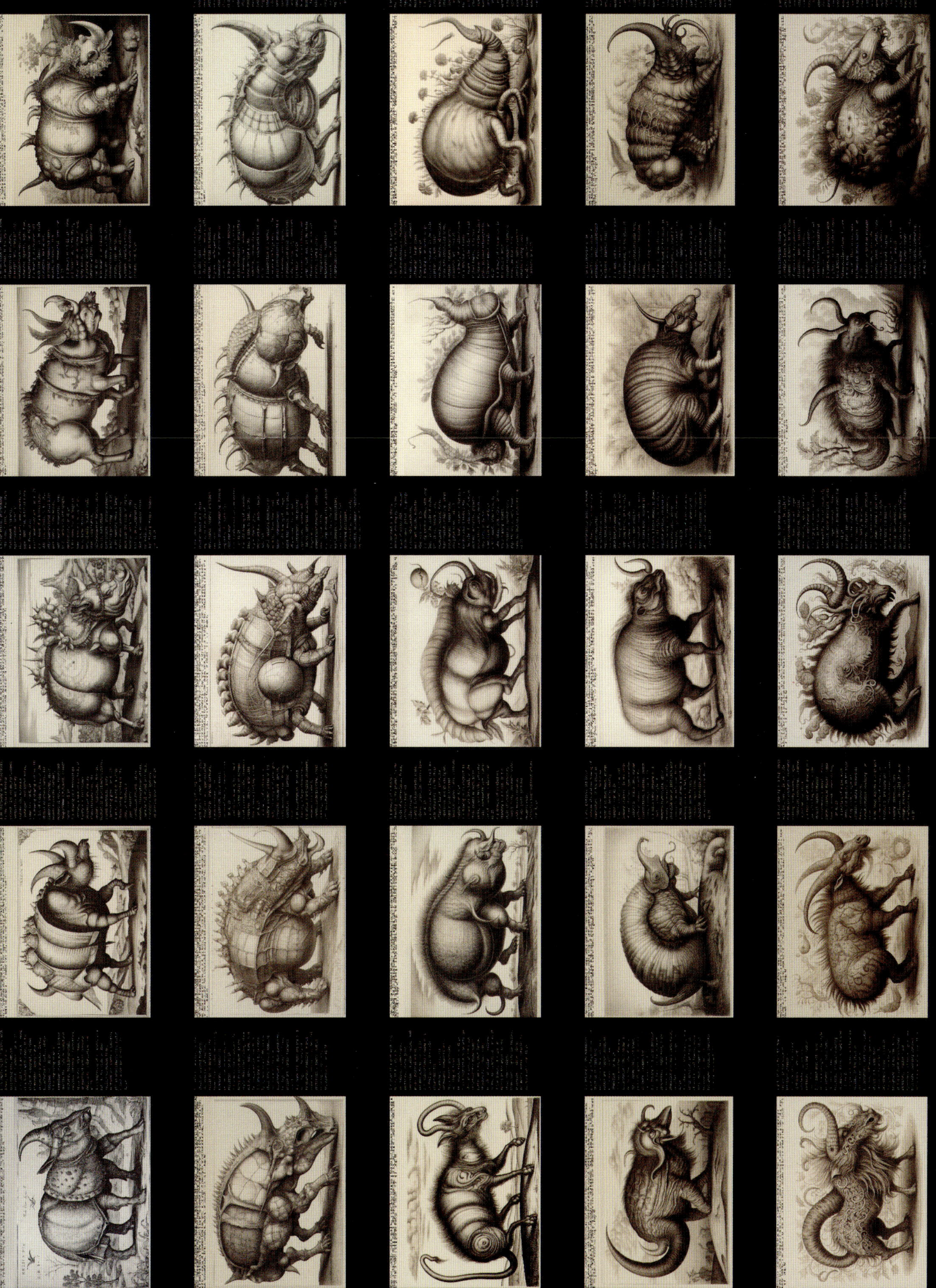

未命名　在具体的创作中，你是如何理解人工智能的？

张　ChatGPT 的出现使得人工智能的使用更加平民化，我现在的创作如果涉及到编程，大部分基础工作都可以在 ChatGPT 里完成。这样的话，我可以将更多的精力放在内容上，创作的周期也会缩短。

当我们问“什么是人工智能”的时候，我们可以通过思考“什么不是人工智能”来确定它的边界。因此在我的毕业创作里，我将人类创作的艺术作品与人工智能创作的图像进行对照，丢勒及其后世艺术家创作出的犀牛组成了一个图集网络，人工智能在算法的引导下也生成了一个新的犀牛图集网络。当它们并置在一起的时候，就可能触发一些思考。

文艺复兴时期的人们面对不同版本的犀牛会陷入困惑，今天的人类看着密密麻麻的 AI 犀牛，或许也会陷入迷茫。历史仿佛是个轮回。人工智能出现之后，大众媒体上出现了很多讨论，很多人都在担心未来，因为真和假可能变得无法区分。其实这样的担忧早在文艺复兴时期就已经发生过了。

不过，对于生成式人工智能，也有人会问，如果 AIGC 是程序内的“伪随机”，其生成的内容遵循规律性、必然性，那人类的创作一定就是自由意志的体现吗？

W&M　When you're creating, how do you see the way artificial intelligence fits in your work?

Zhang　The emergence of ChatGPT has made the use of AI more accessible. Nowadays, if my work involves some coding, most of the basics can be handled within the ChatGPT. That lets me focus more on the content of my creation, and it speeds up the whole creative process.

When we talk about "what is artificial intelligence," we can define the boundaries of the answer by thinking about "what isn't artificial intelligence." Therefore, in my graduation project, I compared human-created artworks with AI-generated images. I connected the rhinoceroses crafted by Dürer and other subsequent artists into a network of collected images, and, under algorithm guidance, I let AI create another network of rhinoceros images. When I put them side by side, it may trigger some thinking.

Back in the Renaissance, people may get confused when confronted with different versions of rhinoceroses. Today, when people look at loads of AI-generated rhinoceroses, they might also feel a bit lost. History seems to be cyclical. After the advent of artificial intelligence, there has been much discussion in the media, and many people are concerned about the future because the line between truth and falsehood may become blurred. But the truth is such concerns date way back to the Renaissance.

Now, about generative AI, some may also wonder if AIGC is "pseudo-random" within the program, and because its generated content follows regularities and inevitabilities, does that mean human creativity necessarily embodies free will?

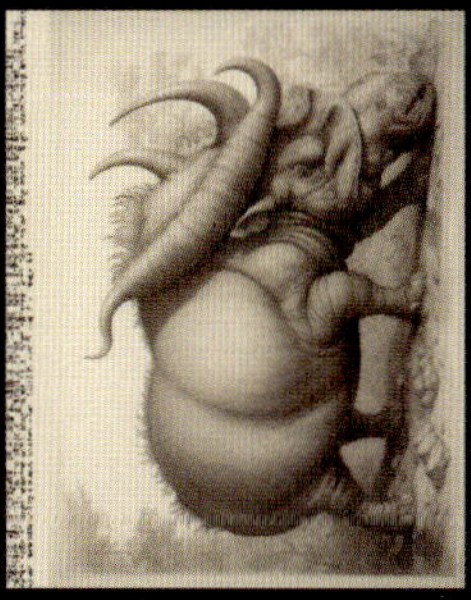

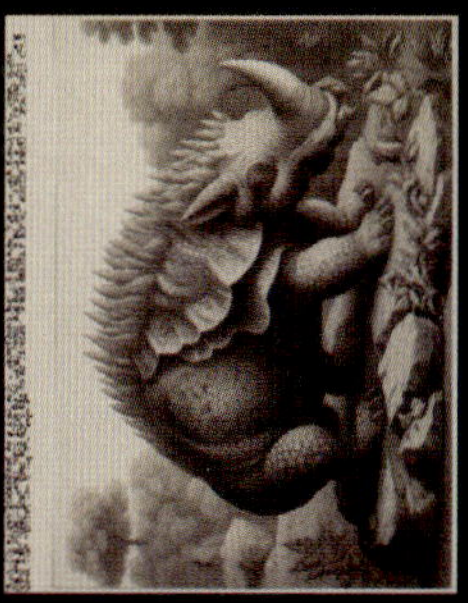

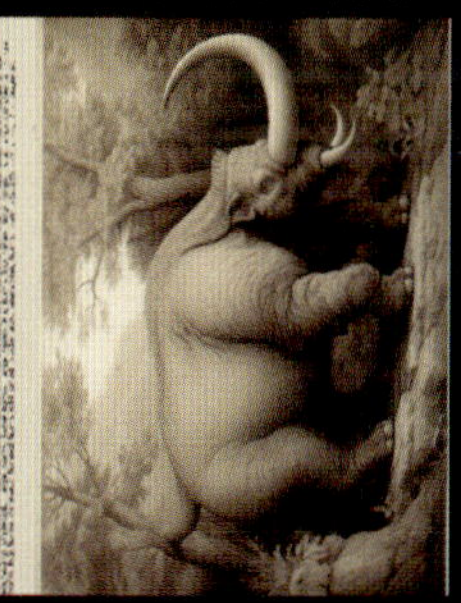
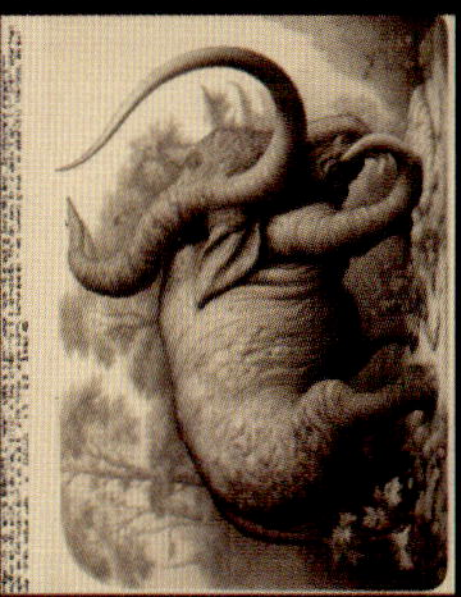

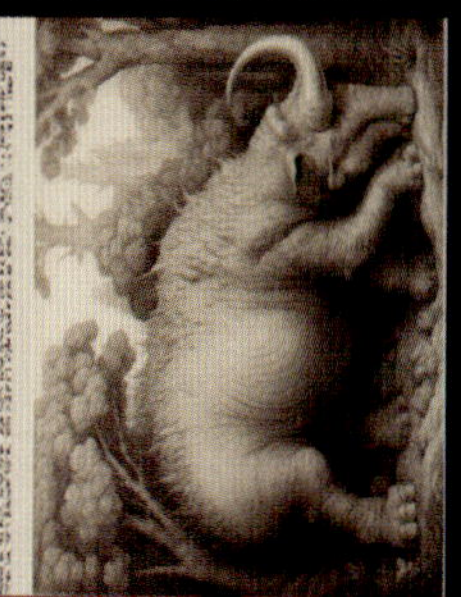

未命名 **丢勒晚年都在思考艺术与数学的关系，这组关系似乎在今天成了人工智能艺术的核心。**

张 我在研究丢勒的时候，翻阅了一些材料，丢勒认为自己并不懂数学，他只是在追求美，美对他来说是真理性的存在。后来他去意大利旅行，他试着用“万物皆数”的方式去理解世界，距离真理也更近了。

我曾经跟西湖大学研究人工智能的朋友聊过天，他们很早就给我介绍了 ChatGPT 的发展，那会儿它还没有正式对外发布。我完全不知所云，就跟丢勒当年对数学的困惑是一样的。

W&M In his later years, Dürer was always pondering the relationship between art and mathematics, and these connections seem to have become the core of AI art today.

Zhang During my research on Dürer, I went through some materials. Dürer believed he wasn't good at math; he was simply pursuing beauty, which, to him, was the existence of truth. Later, during his trip to Italy, he tried to understand the world through the lens of "everything is a number," and that brings him closer to his truth.

I once chatted with friends at West Lake University who were doing research in the field of artificial intelligence. They introduced me to the development of ChatGPT early on, even before its official release. I was utterly puzzled at that time, feeling a bit like Dürer must have felt about mathematics back in the day.

未命名 **他们会跟你分享对艺术的看法吗？**

张 当时西湖大学的科研团队计划推出一款 AIGC 软件，想找几位学艺术的同学聊聊，我很幸运地参与了，也有幸结识了一线的软件工程师。软件工程师是从功能性的角度来理解艺术的，想让 AI 制作出梵高式的绘画。但这里就出现了一个人工智能非常难解决的问题——艺术作品的风格。拉斐尔和达芬奇的艺术风格究竟有什么不同，现阶段的人工智能还是很难给出令人满意的答案。

W&M Did they share their views on art with you?

Zhang At that time, the research team at West Lake University was planning to launch an AIGC software and wanted to chat with a few students studying fine arts. I was fortunate enough to be part of it and had the chance to meet some frontline software engineers. Software engineers tend to understand art from a functional perspective, aiming to get AI to create paintings in the style of Van Gogh. However, a significant challenge arises here—the style of artistic works. Deciphering the differences in artistic styles between Raphael and da Vinci is still a tough task for current AI.

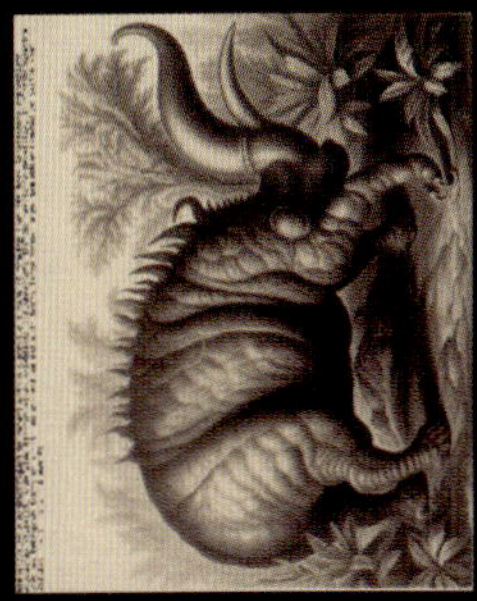

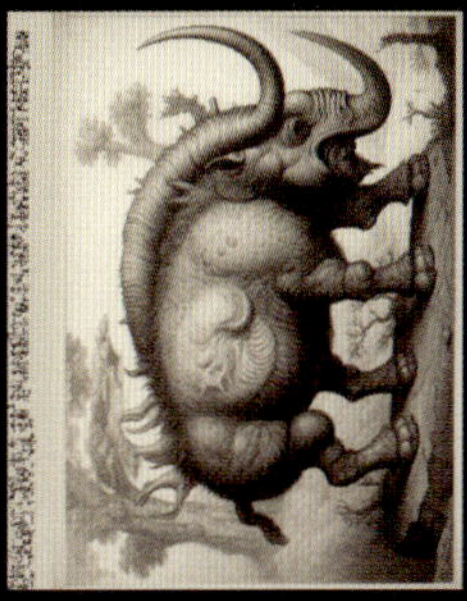
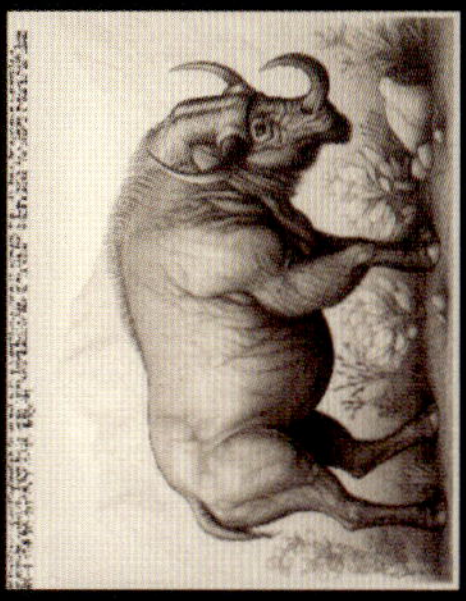

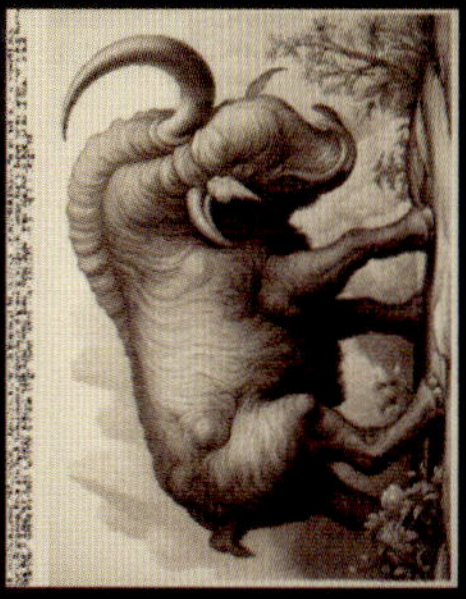

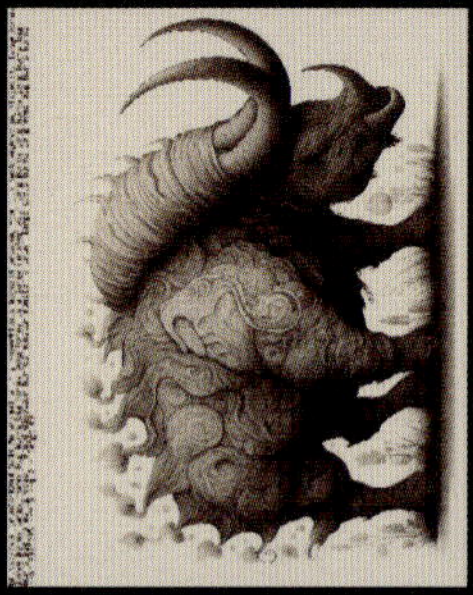

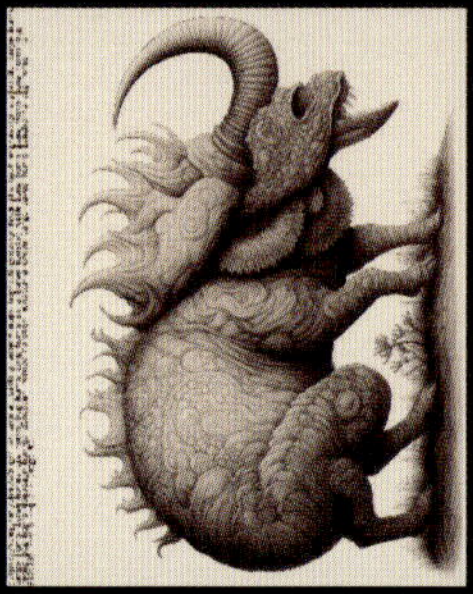

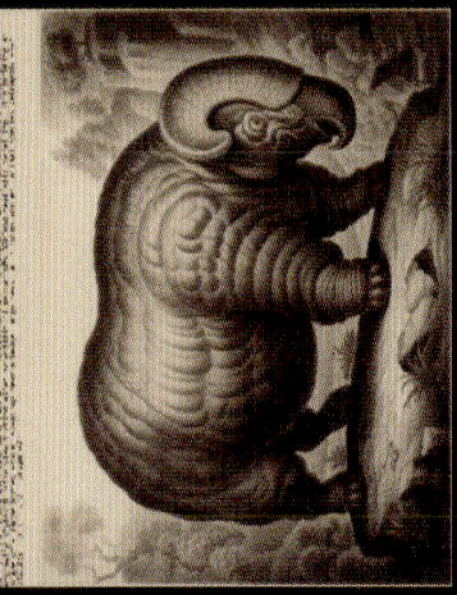

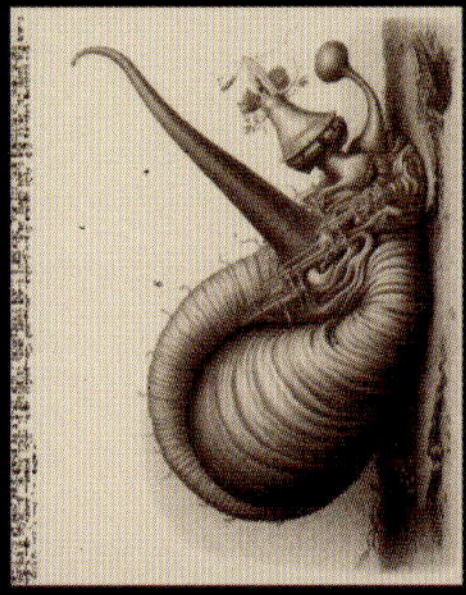

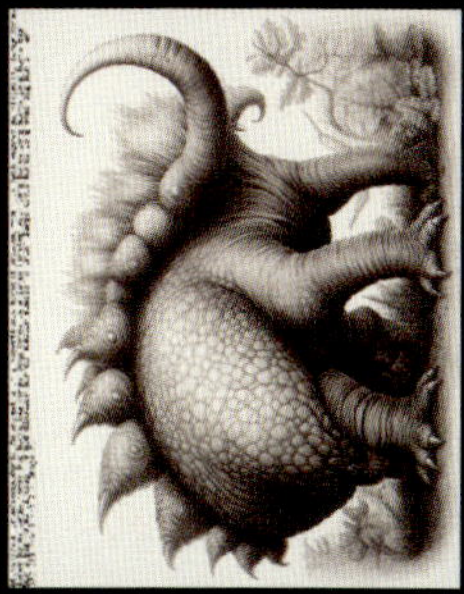

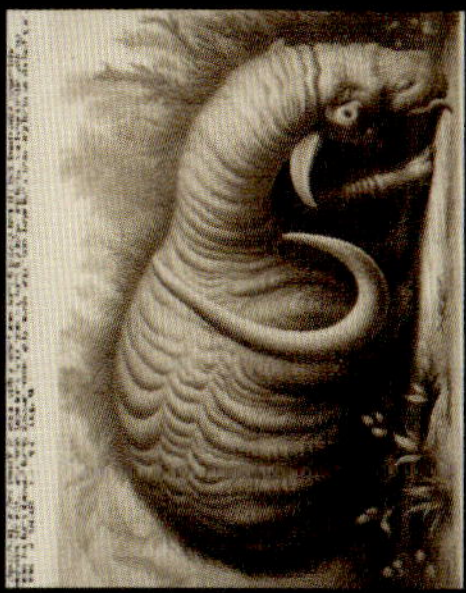

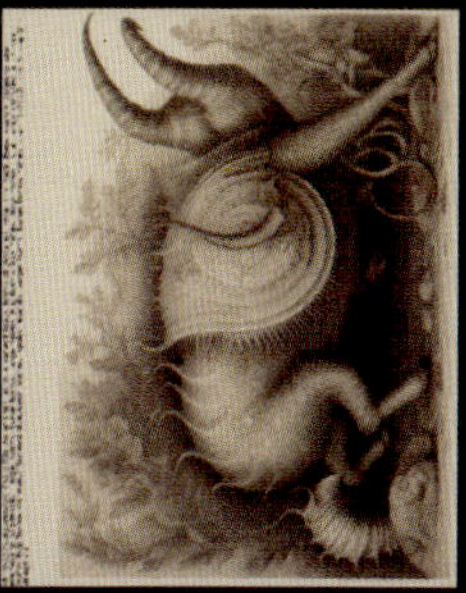
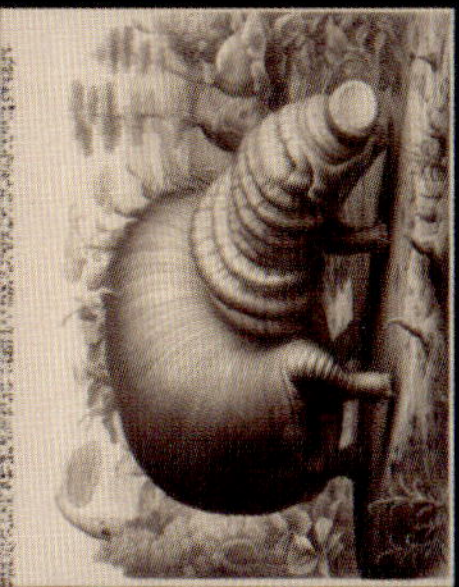

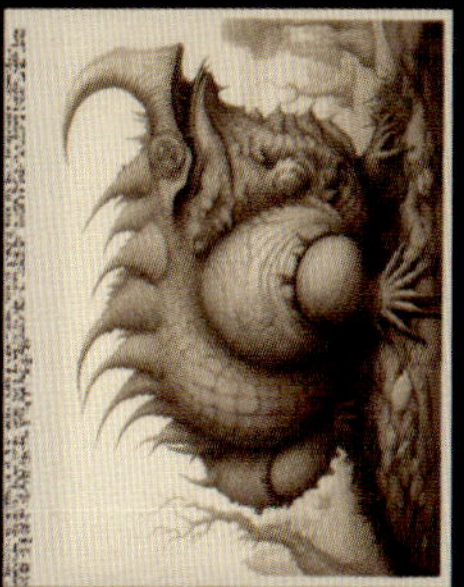

未命名 **传统的艺术创作，艺术家必须不断磨练自己的技艺，而在人工智能时代，艺术家似乎只需要创意，或者说他们把更多的时间花在了数据库和算法模型上。**

张 表面上看，技术的确解放了人的双手，但艺术表达的难度却没有因此减少。马塞尔·杜尚、约瑟夫·博伊斯都是制作现成品艺术的大师，但在他们之后，“人人都是艺术家”的时代似乎并没有到来。

艺术创作注定要依赖媒介，就像人类必须通过“语言”才能思考，英文母语者和中文母语者的思维习惯一定是有区别的。艺术创作同样也在用艺术语言、艺术媒介去思考。版画创作者看待世界的角度会受印刷媒介的影响，数字创作者则可能更偏向用算法程序去模拟推演问题。不论是传统的艺术家，还是新兴媒介的艺术家，他们面对的问题是一样的，都需要不断磨练自己的技艺，无非是木刻刀和计算机软件的区别。

对艺术家而言，仅仅掌握技术是远远不够的，必须创作作品，为变动的社会提供多元的思考。从我个人角度出发，我更希望自己像丢勒，或是达芬奇那样，既精于艺术又懂技术。

W&M In traditional art creation, artists must constantly hone their skills. But in this age of artificial intelligence, artists seem only to need creativity, or in other words, they invest more time in databases and algorithm models.

Zhang At first glance, technology has indeed freed human hands, but the difficulty of expressing artistically has not diminished as a result. Masters like Marcel Duchamp and Joseph Beuys were experts in creating ready-made art. However, after them, the era of “everyone is an artist” seems not to have arrived.

Art creation is destined to rely on some kind of medium, much like how humans must think in a “language”—and English speakers and Chinese speakers also undoubtedly have distinct thinking habits. Artistic creation also engages in thinking through the language and medium of art. Printmakers see the world in ways shaped by the printing medium, while digital creators might prefer to use algorithmic programs to simulate and deduce problems. Whether people are old-school artists or artists utilizing emerging mediums, they're wrestling with the same problems, just with a distinction between a woodcut knife and computer software.

For artists, just mastering technology is far from enough; they must create works that offer diversified thinking for this changing society. Personally speaking, I would prefer to be like Dürer or da Vinci— proficient in both art and technology.

未命名 **人工智能所拥有的决策权力似乎是艺术家主动出让的，但我们对此并没有保持警醒。**

张 AI 可以在某些方面辅助和增强艺术创作，但是否会消解艺术家的主体性，扼杀他们的创造力，则是一个不能简单回答的问题。在今天这个时代，虽然 AI 可以生成艺术作品，但艺术家的思维、情感和生活经历很难被完全模拟或替代。现阶段的 AI 更可能成为工具，帮助艺术家探索新的创意领域，而不是完全取代他们。艺术家的主体性可能会被重新定义，但未必是消解。

W&M It feels like that artist handed over their power of decision-making to artificial intelligence willingly, but we people haven't been too vigilant about it.

Zhang AI can be helpful to assists and enhance the process of artistic creation in certain aspects. But whether it's gonna erode the subjectivity of artists and squash their creativity is a tricky question. In today's world, even though AI can generate artworks, the thoughts, emotions, and life experiences of artists are tough to be fully simulated or replaced. At this point, AI seems more like a tool, assisting artists in exploring new creative territories rather than snatching their jobs entirely. The subjectivity of artists may be redefined, but not necessarily eliminated.

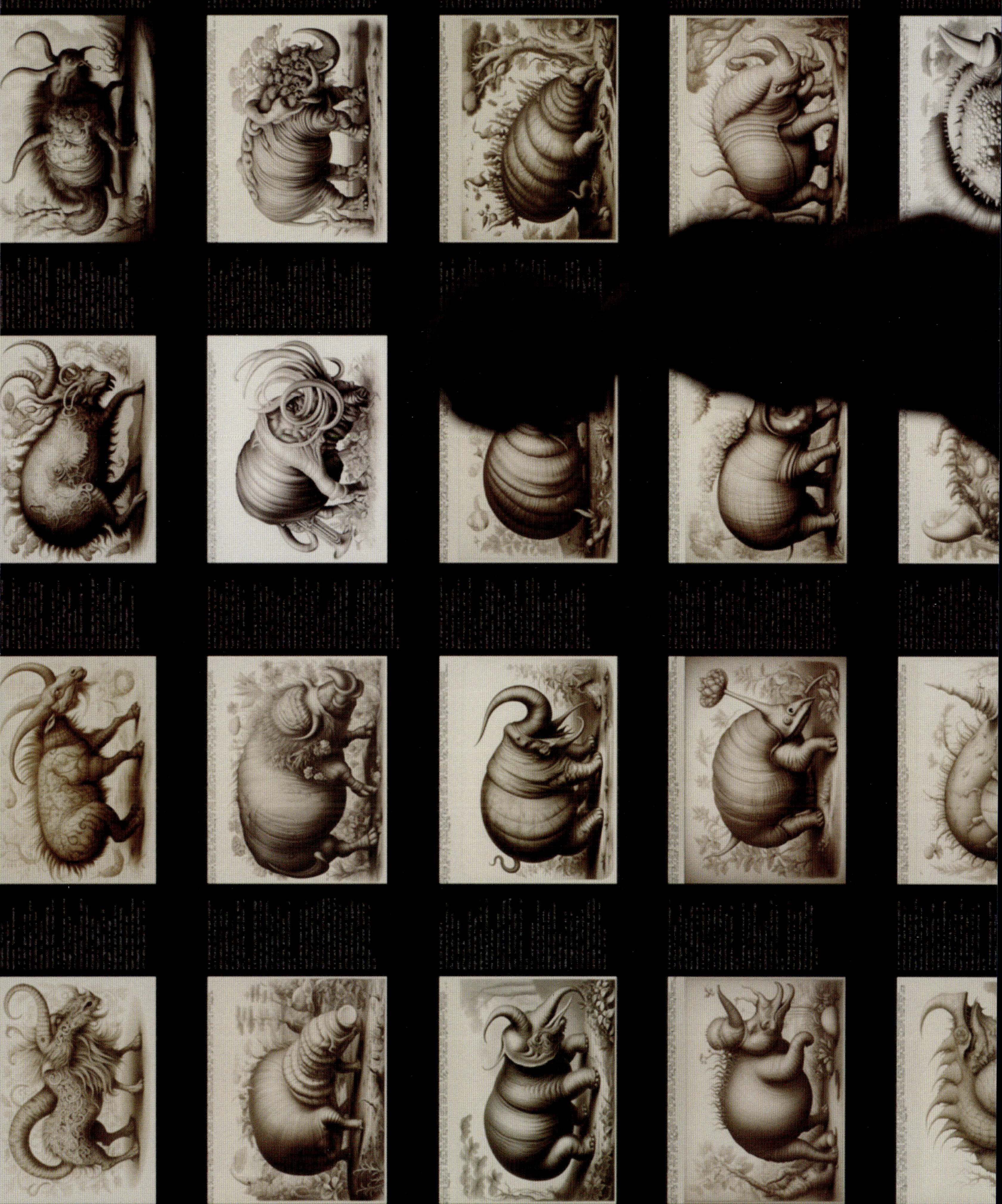

未命名　AI 艺术关注的领域越来越抽象，艺术家个体身上的情感温度在逐渐冷却。你会为此担忧吗？

张　如果这就是当下的事实，就有一点像地球一定会毁灭，无所谓坚持或放弃，“毁灭你与你无关” 嘛，人类只有接受的份。人类还是很顽强的，甚至要去创造元宇宙和移民太空。不过如果真到了那一刻，我的立场应该是刘慈欣在《三体》里写的那样，“给岁月以文明，而不是给文明以岁月。”

W&M　While the focus of AI painting is becoming increasingly abstract, it seems that the individual artists' emotional intensity toward art creation is gradually cooling off. Does that make you worried?

Zhang　If that's the reality nowadays, it's a bit like our Earth is inevitably going to be destroyed – whether you persist in living or give up, “the world ending has nothing to do with you,” you know? Humanity has to accept it. I think humans are still very tenacious, even wanting to create the Metaverse or relocate to space. However, if it really comes to that moment, my stance should be the same as Liu Cixin wrote in *The Three-Body Problem*, “Make time for civilization, for civilization won't make time.”

未命名　你怎么看自己的生活与艺术创作之间的关系？

张　我的创作灵感很少来自于直接的生活经验，往往在我畅想未来的时候，它就出现了。如果是具体的创作，那更多的还是从研究中展开的。

工作之余，我其实是一个一级方程式赛车（F1）车迷。对我来说，F1 的比赛周也算是个两周一次的休息仪式。某种意义上，我把 F1 车手视为艺术家，F1 赛车呈现了一种艺术的终极状态，车手拥有高超的驾驶技术，完美地控制着赛车的运行。F1 比起别的运动更加讲究精确，讲究数学的美感，每一圈要有最精确的刹车点，换胎最短到 1.82 秒，车手根据轮胎的情况，会精准地预测在十圈之后的第几个弯去超越前面的对手。对我来说，这绝对是美的。F1 的团队协作就像是跨学科的艺术合作，车手和赛车的平衡就像艺术与技术的平衡。

W&M　How do you see the connection between your life and artistic creation?

Zhang　My creative inspiration rarely comes directly from life experiences; more often, it pops up when I'm daydreaming about the future. And when I'm doing a specific project, my inspiration usually stems from research.

Outside of my creation work, I'm actually a big Formula 1 (F1) fan. For me, an F1 race weekend is like a bi-weekly ritual of relaxation. In a way, I see F1 drivers as artists; F1 racing embodies the ultimate form of artistry, with drivers showcasing top-notch driving skills, and flawlessly controlling the car's movements. F1 is more about precision than other sports, emphasizing the beauty of mathematics. Each lap needs the most precise braking point, and tire changes in as short as 1.8 to 2.2 seconds. Based on tire conditions, drivers can accurately predict when to overtake opponents after ten laps. To me, that's pure beauty. The team collaboration in the F1 race resembles interdisciplinary cooperation in creating art pieces, and the balance between the driver and the car mirrors the balance between art and technology.

未命名　关于未来的创作，你有什么新的规划吗？

张　具体的创作还是会和人工智能有关，但我觉得目前最重要的事情还是融入到社会之中，从艺术的象牙塔走出来，从南山校区的门口走到西湖边，去跟真实的人和世界打交道。如果说凌晨的西湖是我的幻想世界，那白天的西湖则是我要去面对和学习的真实世界。

W&M　So, what's your plan for future creations?

Zhang　My future projects will still relate to artificial intelligence, but I believe the most crucial thing for me right now is to integrate into society. I need to step out of the ivory tower of art, walk from the entrance of the Nanshan campus to the West Lake, and engage with real people and the real world. If the predawn West Lake is my fantasy world, then the daytime West Lake is the real world I need to face and learn more from.

《Rhino+》
（由 200 幅犀牛图像叠加而成）
AIGC
尺寸可变
2023 年

Rhino+
（Overlaying 200 rhino images）
AIGC
Dimension Variable
2023

后记

2023 年春天，一颗做书的种子悄然萌发，让《未命名艺术》编辑部的成员们得以相逢。初夏，九位充满激情的艺术家带着他们独特的视角与作品加入了我们，一同培育这颗尚在扎根的“未命名”之树。

回首整本书的创作过程，九位艺术家慷慨地敞开心扉，以各自独特的视角诠释着他们对当代艺术的理解与追求。每位艺术家都曾在创作的漫漫长路上遇到了不尽相同的山峰与深谷，他们的创意与思考，是这本书最珍贵的精神内核。

不同于成熟艺术家的传记材料，这本书中的“对话”发生在创作者们尚未“成名”之前。编辑团队尽可能地隐去“批评”的姿态，而是让作品和艺术家说话。在章节设计中，编辑团队努力捕捉艺术家的创作本色，同时也希望为读者创造出一种层次分明、节奏自然的阅读体验。

“万事开头难”，也许是在这段旅程中听过最多的一句话。《未命名艺术》第一辑的编辑与出版确实留下了些许遗憾：由于版面有限，我们只能择取部分作品，未能完整展现艺术家们的才华。另外，在编辑过程中，部分图片质量未能达到统一标准。一方面是艺术家的创作已经完成，留下的影像资料有限；另一方面，也是因为编辑团队介入太晚，未能深入艺术家的创作现场。还有些出色的艺术家因为出国深造等原因未能参与本书的创作，但编辑部已与他们建立了联系，相信在今后的出版中，这些年轻的艺术家终将与读者相遇。书中其他不足之处，恳请读者批评指正。

与艺术家和读者朋友们共同创造，始终是我们编辑部秉持的理念。衷心感谢所有帮助过《未命名艺术》的朋友，正是你们为这颗“未命名”的种子提供了茁壮成长的沃土。希望《未命名艺术》在未来的时间里超越书籍这一媒介，为艺术家和读者搭建一个平台。在这里大家可以连接彼此，分享艺术之爱。

《未命名艺术》编辑部

Afterword

In the spring of 2023, the seed of a book quietly sprouted and brought together the members of the Waking & Making editorial team. By early summer, nine passionate artists joined us with their unique perspectives and works, working alongside us to nurture this budding Waking & Making tree as it took root.

Looking back on the creation of this book, the nine artists generously shared their hearts and offered a unique perspective on their understanding and pursuit of contemporary art. Along their creative journeys, marked by individual peaks and valleys, their insights and ideas shape the true essence of this book.

Unlike biographical material of established artists, the "dialogues" in this book capture the creators before they "gained recognition". We chose to step back from a "critical" stance, allowing the works and artists to speak for themselves. In designing the chapters, the editorial team has aimed to capture the genuine essence of each artist's work while creating a reading experience that is layered and flows with a natural rhythm.

"The first step is always the hardest" was perhaps the most frequently heard phrase during this journey. The publication of the first volume of Waking & Making inevitably left a few regrets; we could only select certain works and couldn't fully showcase the artists' talents with limited space. Some images lacked consistent quality during editing, since the artists' works were already completed, we had limited visual materials and joining the process late made it difficult to fully engage with their creative environments. And some outstanding artists were unable to participate in the publication of this book due to reasons such as studying abroad, but the editorial team has been in touch with them. We believe that future publications will provide opportunities for these exceptional young artists to connect with readers. As we strive to refine our work, we sincerely welcome any criticism and suggestions from our readers regarding any other shortcomings of this book.

Co-creating with artists and readers is the core concept of our editorial team. We extend our heartfelt thanks to everyone who supported the creation of Waking & Making; your support has provided the fertile ground for this young seed to grow. We hope that in the future, Waking & Making will transcend the medium of books and build a platform for artists and readers, where people can connect and share their love for art.

Waking & Making